What I Learned From 50 CELEBRITIES

(By screwing up in front of them)

FARRELL HIRSCH

D1412522

For more information contact:
Riverdale Avenue Books
5676 Riverdale Avenue
Riverdale, NY 10471

www.riverdaleavebooks.com

Design by www.formatting4U.com
Cover by Scott Carpenter

Digital ISBN: 9781626014596

Print ISBN: 9781626014589

First Edition August, 2018

Table of Contents

An Introduction

Here's what I did in this book, just so you know; much of what I have learned in life is the result of my interactions with well-known people. These really are the stories of how I changed, and these famous people really were the catalysts. Most of these stories I've told at parties and have been asked to repeat again, partly because they are valuable morality tales and partly because they involve me making as ass of myself in front of celebrities.

In my mind, the names involved in these stories make them repeatable and, hopefully, more memorable. The intent is that you will internalize the lessons that I did.

If I didn't learn anything from the encounter, it didn't make the book. There's no mention of the time I met a teenaged Eddie Murphy, or the time Conan O'Brien seemed to want to beat me out of a free meal.

One thing to pay attention to here is that there are no stories where the celebrity is abusive or evil. These are the stories where I was the ass and embarrassed myself. That's why I think of this book as a self-help book, and not a memoir. And I am the idiot, whose self it mostly helped.

This isn't a linear story of my life, just little disparate anecdotes that form a mosaic.

On the following page you will see a list of chapters, each with the name of a celebrity who was the star of the story that enlightened me. I had thought that before reading it, you might enjoy seeing the list of another 100 or so celebrities who get mentioned in this book, but do not have their own chapters. An appetizer before the main course.

Conan O'Brien, Robin Thicke, Bugsy Siegel, Kevin Spacey, George Takei, Dwayne "The Rock" Johnson, Abe Lincoln, Hulk Hogan, Al Gore, Tony Bennett, Lil Jon, Yankees manager Joe Girardi, Warren Moon, John Belushi, Tom Jones, Lech Wałęsa, Mariette Hartley, Ed Begley Jr., Faye Dunaway, Bruno Sammartino, Dudley Moore, Scott Baio, Nicollette Sheridan, Maria Callas, porn star Christy Canyon, Mickey Mouse, Chelsea Handler, Ron and Nancy Reagan, Pharaoh Ramses II, Shecky Greene, Adele, Broadway legend Elaine Stritch, Michael Phelps, Moses, Knute Rockne, Richard Petty, NBA Hall-of-Famer Rick Barry, Megyn Kelly, Merv Griffin, Ben Hur, Studs Terkel, Barbra Streisand, Neil Diamond, Dinah Shore, piano virtuoso Van Cliburn, Gilda Radner, Mandy Patinkin, Tim Robbins, Phillip Seymour Hoffman, Henrik Ibsen, Eydie Gormé, Nature Boy Ric Flair, Sir John Gielgud, Frank Sinatra, Lee Harvey Oswald, Roger Federer, Tom Waits, Barack Obama, Carly Simon, vice presidential candidate John Edwards, Jean-Claude Van Damme, Lord Byron, Dr. Drew, The Mighty Morphin' Power Rangers, The Kardashians, Betty Grable, Laraine Newman, Bow Wow, Macaulay Culkin, Gavin Rossdale, Deborah Harry, Patrick Stewart, The Ramones, Tom Hanks, The Sex Pistols, Bea Arthur and Denzel Washington.

I was a stubborn young man who believed that he

was smarter than just about everyone, in just about every circumstance. Somehow along the way I still managed to live just about every dream a 13 year-old boy could have. I have written a play that I got to watch on stage at Lincoln Center, I worked with the coaching staff of a professional sports team. I partied at the Playboy Mansion. I had spent years developing national radio programming heard by millions and launched the careers of some pretty big stars. I was even the executive producer of a celebrity filled-awards show, and I once got to work at a nudist swingers resort in Jamaica.

That last one was just bragging. This book is really my journey to understanding my own idiocy— and I will get back to that thought in a moment. First, let me tell you what else this book is.

It's an apology. Quite literally an apology to a whole list of celebrities I offended and disregarded, even though most of them won't even remember the incident. This book is a celebrity tell-all—where every celebrity is the good guy and nobody, save me, has their intimacy trampled.

And that's why I had to leave out a story about John McEnroe backstage at a charity event in the late 70's. And the one where I had to play drums for Billy Idol for four minutes. And the one where Bette Midler and Martha Stewart were very nice to me, but someone else wasn't.

This book is also a roadmap for all the other blowhards and the self-righteous people having trouble getting out of their own way. People might turn to you often and say, "Oh, please. Just get over yourself" but nobody really tells you how to do that. What are the steps to getting over one's self?

I know, and I will tell you.

Don't you despise the smug and dismissive "Been there, done that," retort? I suggest that the reason you dislike it so intensely is that it presupposes that there is no need for explanation or detail. No matter what situation might arise in your life, the answer on how to handle it is in this book. It isn't enough for me to say that I've been there and done that. I've taken on the job of writing out the exact details, explaining my mistake and telling you what I have learned. This is where I've been, and this is what I have done.

Getting through that threshold, where career-ending and relationship-threatening mistakes were a regular occurrence, and being able to look back through the looking glass and see my own stupidity has led me to some conclusions.

I don't blame my mother and father. They tried. The parents of my failures were arrogance and obstinance. I did not have much use for the wisdom of teachers, experts, professionals or anyone else. That wasn't teenage rebellion or punk philosophy, it was merely my misguided worldview.

I was never a kid who caused malicious damage. I was more prone to the long-term damage done to my own future goals by self-inflicted wounds. I was a kid who was asked in first grade by the principal, "What did you learn today?" And I answered, "Today I learned the teacher thinks that the Earth is round." The Principal responded, "Don't you think the earth is round?" And of course I said, "Yep, but I already knew that. Today I learned *the teacher* thinks the earth is round." Insufferable.

When I moved to Los Angeles to become a

writer, I refused a job on a TV show as an intern because I thought, "Then they're always going to think of me that way." I refused to take a class on proper screenwriting form because that was "for the people without talent." And time after time I did not honor the relationships of potential mentors.

I was an idiot.

And maybe you, or someone you know, is the same kind of idiot.

Today? Oh today I am assuredly wiser and more self-aware… to know one's idiocy is to salvage one's soul from it. Nothing in this book is revolutionary. Every lesson you can learn from it is something you could have learned from a parent, a grandparent, or even a good book. Unless you're an idiot.

But here's the catch. Idiots don't know they are idiots. That's the wonderful irony-loop of sustained lifelong idiocy. And if you laugh at that, at those idiots, secure that you are not one. then you probably are. Of course, really accepting that you are a victim of idiocy also indicates that you probably aren't one anymore.

Got that?

Ok, back to the book.

Farrell Hirsch
August 2018

Chapter One
Lisa Kudrow

Background

In the summer of 1980 Lisa Kudrow and I were between our junior and senior years of high school on opposite ends of the country. There was little reason to meet. Lisa attended a Cornell University summer program that July with several of her friends. I did not. There still wasn't much reason to think we would meet. But a few of my buddies also attended those same weeks in Ithaca and *my* New York guys befriended *her* LA Valley girls.

In October of that year, my buddies and I travelled across the country to visit Lisa, and her friends (Liz, Nancy, Lori and Allison) and mine started a really wonderful and adventurous interconnected web of teenage friendships. You know Lisa Kudrow as the somewhat wacky ditz of the *Friends* girls. But that's the TV filter of a world where everyone is impossibly beautiful and fascinating. To a man (though we were truly just boys) we saw Lisa as an exotic, statuesque beauty with a gifted intellect, and the poise and presence that made you want to introduce her to your grandmother as your fiancée.

1

Story

Lisa and I were never remarkably close, but we did stay in touch through the 1980s. I even visited her for a few hours at Vassar—though my only recollection of that time was that she was slightly distracted by my presence and showed me a tree that was supposed to impress me. I don't know why, but I remember she was way too involved in showing me a specific Vassar tree.

As that decade was ending, Lisa was both performing in the Groundlings and doing her own improv show called Plan B at a 40-seat theatre in Hollywood. It was clear that she was both talented and funny, and I had not expected that to be the case. I only knew her as very reserved.

At that same time I had written my first play, called *Different States,* and though I still like it (and it did pretty well) it very much feels like a first play. One of the lead characters, Astrid, was a wild, exotic, sexy fantasy of a woman who my stage directions described as "a free spirited seductress of both humanity and ideas."

I asked Lisa to read the role of Astrid in a reading at my West Hollywood apartment so I could hear the play outside of my own head. No rehearsal. No audience. Just myself and four actors sitting around on psychedelic couches inherited from my grandmother. Lisa was brilliant.

She got every joke as she was reading it for the first time. She played wonderfully off Dana Stevens as they debated who was actually each other's alter ego. And here's the important part. Watching this I was convinced I was saving her—discovering her—presenting her to the world.

Watching her improv show, in skit after skit I saw her do variations on the same theme; the well-intentioned dingbat. I was instantly convinced she could do so much more. So when we raised enough money to present a full production of *Different States*, she was my first call. I didn't even have a director yet.

I officially offered her the role and even offered to have her help me choose the director. Boom! She turned me down almost immediately. She was kind enough to say that she was a fan of the writing (and I am insecure enough to cherish the compliment) but that she had a plan for her career and this particular role wasn't the kind of thing that fit into her vision of the character portfolio she was constructing.

I did what any pompous young writer would do; I told her she was crazy. We were taking the show to New York and that level of exposure was so far superior to her little Plan B stint that she was practically throwing away her career. I might not have said it out loud but I was thinking, "There are a million ditzy waitress types in L.A., and why aspire to a career that has a ceiling as the wacky sitcom neighbor?"

Livid and indignant, I shook my head in figurative condescension at how she was tossing aside so cavalierly what might be her one golden ticket.

A couple of years later I saw her on *Cheers* as Woody's girlfriend's pal. Nice for her, but that's a top limit.

And then there she was on some sitcom with Bob Newhart. Cool. But similar.

Mad About You… Friends… Movie roles, producing gigs…

I am fairly sure she feels today that she made the right choice.

3

Lesson

"To Thine Own Self Be True." A quarter of a century ago Lisa had a vision of her future. It was a very specific, well thought out plan that really incorporated her best assets. A less evolved person (me, for instance) would have jumped at every morsel of imagined opportunity. While nobody has a path to success that is an absolutely straight line, the brilliance of Lisa Kudrow was that her plan had a predetermined end point. She didn't say, "I want to be an actress." She didn't say, "I want to be on TV" or "I want to be rich and famous." She said, "There is a specific kind of role for which I am well-suited. I will apply maximum efforts toward perfecting all the different aspects that go into creating that kind of talent and that kind of career.

There's a temptation to say "But had she broadened the scope, maybe she could have been a Meryl Streep, why didn't she take the Streep approach?" I don't know Streep at all. But I would bet dollars to donuts that Meryl did the exact same thing that Lisa did. As Kudrow put it, "I envision that my future is as a chameleon." And I would bet she spent every waking moment perfecting the tools to achieve that goal, and more importantly, discarding the crap that distracted from the finish line.

I tell this story as I mentor radio hosts these days. I see people getting lost as "generalists." The better advice is to look for your niche. Find it at the intersection of your talents and your interests and make that the street corner at which you plant your flag. Once established, you can wander from it before returning home. But unless you establish that foundation, you are simply wandering.

Addendum

I hope you can tell that I have both affection and respect for Lisa. And I am reticent to overstate our friendship. So let me state for the record that the last time I saw her was during her time on *Mad About You*. I had an appointment on that lot and was stuck at the gate because my name was left off a list. She happened to wander by with co-star Leila Kenzle, vouched for me when it would have been simpler to avoid the situation, and I got to my meeting. The time before that was at the bris of a young man who is currently a college student, and the time before that was when we were in the same wedding party on July 20th 1987, when I think her date was her good friend Conan O'Brien (which is the precursor to a Conan story that should have been included in this book).

Chapter Two
Hugh Hefner

Background

I worked for Playboy for about ten years, I ran a division for them and was extremely proud of the product and our success. Even though I had no experience around playmates or radio, I was hired in 2002 to create and run Playboy Radio—a new station on the cutting edge of the emerging technology that was satellite radio.

The brand was somewhat past its prime, but that bunny logo still had a phenomenal worldwide recognition factor, and the company had incredible tentacles. They had a book publishing wing, a recording label, the Playboy Clubs, the Playboy Jazz Festival, the iconic magazine and a successful TV network. There were a plethora of places from which to draw content, but I often bragged that I was able to take the world's most visual brand into the world's least visual medium; radio. It's cool to have a catch phrase.

During my first week on the job I read that Mr. Hefner was in his 80's. I went to my boss at the time—an incredibly nice man who just had the demeanor and characteristics of a hit man for the 1930's mob. His presence was so imposing that people avoided him in the hallways, but he was a wonderfully competent and generous boss. I was considering the potential longevity of my new position and asked "So what happens to the company if Mr. Hefner dies?" He answered, "His mother lived to 109, so don't make any plans." That speaks to both the reverence in which Hef was held by long-time employees, and the longevity of his relevance. Hef was a spark of the sexual revolution, an innovator in publishing, a campaigner for free speech and a pioneer in racial equality. Combine all of that with the mystique of his famous parties with their endless parades of women... There never will be another Hef.

Story

Traditionally the Playmate of the Year announcement was done in the spring, at the Mansion. It was always a luncheon for press and a reunion for all Playmate sisters to come back home and get reacquainted, but Playboy's fortunes had turned somewhat by the time of this story and the priority had become trying to maximize the financial return of every single iota of publicity.

Playboy had opened the first of what they hoped would become a new wave of Playboy Clubs at the Palms Hotel in Las Vegas. The hotel's owners, the Maloof Brothers, were fans and appreciators of the brand Mr. Hefner had built and were only too happy to have their performance venue become the new home of the Playmate of the Year Announcement. That, of course, became a very different event. Mr. Hefner's serene, erudite, garden luncheon was scrapped in favor of a glitzy, star-studded, televised, red carpet event. My Playboy Radio team was right there with live red carpet coverage of all the proceedings. Our morning host Kevin Klein was the MC, Robin Thicke performed, and the paparazzi paparized.

But our story actually happened on the red carpet. We were shorthanded, and even though I was the executive in charge of the programming, I also had some duties usually given to the interns.

At this point I had been in a room—or at a meeting—with Hef maybe a dozen times. I vividly remember the one time his secretary called and asked me to come over to the Mansion for a meeting. That's an hour-long drive through L.A. mid-day traffic. I remember cursing in the car on the way over. "What the hell does he have to say that he couldn't say on the god damn phone? I can't believe this guy is gonna waste my day driving to his mansion, knowing full well when I get there I'm gonna be ushered into his backyard to wait by his pool, be given a stupid ass drink, and have to watch a bunch of hot naked girls frolic in…" And then it dawned on me: I was the world's most jaded, spoiled ass. If the worst complaint I could muster was that Hef invited me to hang by the pool for an hour in the middle of my workday, I should be grateful. Call this a lesson within a lesson. Be grateful for the things you really do have in front of you. and don't piss them away with anger.

Back to my red carpet, Vegas/Playmate of the Year story.

As Hef and the current group of girlfriends sauntered down the carpet and the flashbulbs popped (or would have popped if this was 1923). I leaned in across the velvet ropes to see who might be next down the carpet so I could alert my broadcast team. I must have encroached upon Hef's field of vision. He spotted me there against the ropes and, bless the guy's heart, not only did he recognize me instantly, he surmised that here I was, one of his valued employees, and I wasn't being allowed into the event. Mr. Hefner never likes to see anyone not ensconced in full party mode. Especially one of *his* boys.

We make eye contact, and he says "Hey." I would then say he forgot my name, but that would be self-flattery. Though he knew exactly who I was, he never actually knew my name. "Hey. Uh... Radio." Which is as good as a name, right? "Radio. Come here." And he motions at me to cross the velvet rope line and approach him. Security unhooks the stanchion and I walk over to him. I see my boss out of the corner of my eye doing that throat slitting motion toward me and mouthing, "Get out of there." But there clearly was no gracious way to accomplish that feat. I was dressed for work, not red carpet, sport coat and wrinkled jeans. If I had planned it I would be dressed down, Hollywood, I-don't-give-a-crap chic. But, no, I was just out of place.

Hef leans over and says, "I got your back."

And we walked in to the party together, Hef... the girlfriends... and me.

As soon as we got through the front door, Hef was satisfied that his good deed had been successfully accomplished and said triumphantly, "You're on your own now, kid." And disappeared into whatever VIP inner sanctum had been set up for him.

Now let me be clear; Hef was not putting on a show for the cameras, of this I am 100% sure. It was simply the open heart of a kind giant who could not stand to see one of *his* people get the shaft. I thanked him, and when he was out of sight I went right back out to the broadcast location.

Lesson

Success comes to those who think with their brains and not with their dicks, even if they're Hugh freakin' Hefner. I'm telling you from a decade working around the man, while nobody would deny his libido was healthy, that wasn't what separated him from the rest of us. In fact, it is what united him with every other American male of his generation. It was the common bond on which his brand was built. But his brain and his hard work are the elements that turned carnal thoughts into an empire.

I used this lesson often in my days running Playboy radio. We could have simply done a station of phone sex and dirty talk, and there most certainly was some of that. But the guiding principle was always, "How can we take that and do more, do better, do different. What can we do that other brands on either side of us couldn't—that's *Esquire* on the classier side, *Penthouse* or *Hustler* on the other.

Addendum

Only once in the years I worked there did we have a company Christmas party at the Mansion. I'd been there for many other events, but there's a pretty sacrosanct rule about sharing stories from *those* evenings. Most of the people who worked on a daily basis for Playboy TV, Playboy Radio and Playboy.com never got the opportunity to meet Hef or hang at the house. That shouldn't seem so unusual, I'm sure most Microsoft employees don't party with Bill and Melinda Gates. So it was a really big deal when we had that office Christmas party in the boss' backyard.

There was a ton of food.

There was enough alcohol.

There was a live band and a dance floor.

And after dessert, there was Hef.

The plan was to have him meet the team, one by one. As people were filing by to shake his hand, I had alternating visions of this being a Papal visitation with a ring kissing ceremony, and then of this being like a department store Santa, and we children asking for a raise for Christmas, or a more flexible vacation schedule for Chanukah.

Interesting thing about Mr. Hefner. Around his friends, his very many, incredibly long-term friends, he was a gregarious yet sincere bon-vivant. With a crowd of virtual strangers who happened to work for him, he was just incredibly shy.

Chapter Three
Leonard Nimoy

Background

I was producing an awards show, The Ovation Awards. That show will come up often in these stories because award shows are simply the best place to acquire one-off celebrity stories. Stars come in for one day, they feel incredibly insecure and will be judged on every aspect of a performance for which they receive neither remuneration nor rehearsal; that is a recipe for good stories.

The Ovation Awards are Los Angeles' only peer judged theatre awards show. The West Coast Tonys, if you will. Though I was around for their birth, their real parents are Larry and Alisa, Jeff, Don, Lars, Bill, Barbara and Tom. By year six of the program I was the executive producer. But that first year there wasn't much hierarchy, we were mostly just a collective. I was clearly near the bottom of the bottom of the nonexistent hierarchy when things started.

For some oddball reason, probably because fate wanted me to write this book, I was put in charge of lining up celebrity presenters. Now you have to understand, the Los Angeles Theatre community has a double inferiority complex. In L.A. we are clear second fiddles to the Movie/TV business, and in the Theatre world we have never had the prestige of New York and Broadway. So big stars, with their egos, and their ever-present need to constantly position themselves, were always a hard sell. "Yes, sir, it is a non-televised award show honoring the best in Los Angeles the... No Mr. Hanks we cannot afford a limo to..." There were many of those types of calls.

As the show grew in prestige and reputation we did better over the years, Kevin Spacey... Annette Bening... but that first year was excruciatingly hard in terms of gaining respect. And to know me is to know that there is no unfulfillable promise I might not make to get a celebrity to attend, and conversely no rude comment I would refrain from if one crossed my imaginary line of respect.

This is the story of a proud earnest man, trying to deal with... me.

Story

I don't have to explain who Leonard Nimoy was. He was, and is, Spock. Imagine being enough of a cultural icon that you knocked the all-time greatest baby doctor, and cultural icon in his own right, off the perch as "Spock." But he had also starred on Broadway, most notably in *Equus*, a play about... the psychiatric treatment of an adolescent who blurs together his sexual development with a worship of horses.

Through some eight-way connection I had managed to get Mr. Nimoy to agree to be a presenter on our inaugural awards show. This was November of 1992 at the Alex Theatre in Glendale. Our hosts that year were Broadway stars John Rubinstein and Joanna Gleason. big names in the theatre world. If you don't know their names, look them up, you will recognize their faces.

About three days out from the show, I finished writing the script of mindless patter each presenter must utter. I print it out on my best 1992 dot matrix printer and fax a copy to each of the presenters. I don't expect much feedback because, first, I included a note letting each know they could later, change and rewrite as they saw fit and second, I really didn't think anyone would look at it until they arrived at the theatre the night of.

My phone rang shortly after sending out the fax, and I picked it up.

"Hello?"

"Farrell, it's Leonard Nimoy."

"Hey Mr. Nimoy, did you get the pages I faxed over?"

"I did. But there seems to be some mistake"

Uh oh. "A mistake? Ok, what's the problem, sir?"

"Farrell, I am an actor."

"Yes sir, Mr. Nimoy, that's not a mistake. Despite what your parents probably warned you about. But you're one of my favorites. I think I already told you that my family took me to see *Equus* when I was eight and…"

"They shouldn't have done that. But here's the thing. I'm an actor, you know"

"Yes…?"

"I should be giving out an acting award."

Ah yes, remember when I mentioned in the background info that performers are always cognizant of their position vis-à-vis other actors? Nimoy had already agreed to do the show over his agent's objection. He had put himself on the line for our show, somewhat, at least as far as his ego went. And from his perspective I was screwing with him. I got that. But I tried to reason with him.

"Mr. Nimoy, I'm sure you understand that putting together a show like this is a crazy jigsaw puzzle. "

"Yes"

"And if you could do us this favor, you know there are so many people to fit in, and so many really gracious people like yourself that…"

"But I'm an actor. I should be giving out an acting award." And he wasn't angry. Just calmly making his case. He seemed confident he could call my bluff. But I couldn't give in without having to just have the conversation with someone else in an hour. So I quickly came up with a sure fire way to respectfully get my point across.

"Mr. Nimoy, who do you think I should bump from the acting category? Annette Bening, or Charlton Heston?"

Got him, right? He was silent for a good long moment. I had him backed into a corner. He *had to* see that my dilemma.

And he said, "Annette Bening."

At that moment I found his answer fully preposterous and considered it a license to speak more freely. Because there's no way I'm bumping Annette freaking Bening for Leonard freaking Nimoy. Especially after what I saw in *Equus*.

"Mr. Nimoy, you have to understand. We specifically chose **you** for the sound awards because of the big pointy Vulcan ears"

Click.

15

Lesson

No, wait, listen. I don't think the lesson here is the one you expect. Although he didn't return my calls for the next few days, Leonard Nimoy showed up to the 1992 Ovation Awards and graciously presented the awards for achievement in sound.

We could call this lesson "Don't be an ass." But you already know that advice and frankly, sometimes you are one, and you usually don't realize it 'til it is too late anyway. So what good is it for me to tell you now?

No. The lesson to learn here is from Leonard Nimoy. He might not like the way I'm choosing to phrase it, but I gave him an impossible dilemma and he gave it the old *Kobayashi Maru* treatment. The lesson here is that the best way out of almost any difficult situation is the logical (go Spock!) and classy path. The hissy fit, the no-show, the making a statement from the stage. These were all paths that would have reflected badly upon him. And though he hated the situation, and me for putting him in it, he rightly surmised (sorry) that the needs of the many outweighed the needs of the one.

These sorts of lessons become invaluable when you have kids. You try to teach them that the goals of the entire family outweigh their particular whim of the moment. No, you can't have bean soup before a cross country car trip, even if it is your favorite— for the good of the family. No, you can't cut up the bed sheets so you can play a tent game for 15 minutes.

Yeah—looks like I got good parenting advice from Mr. Spock. He was a virtual Dr. Spock.

Addendum

Each year's Ovation Awards during the time I was there would open with a video retrospective of the year's best work. And each video opened with a distinctly voiced celebrity saying "Good evening, and welcome to the 1993 Ovation Awards. Here are your nominees."

Theatre folk are many things, all of them diametrically opposed to one another. We are a snooty highbrow bunch, and simultaneously a raucous party in perpetual motion.

In one year, I think 1993, we got George Takei to do the V.O. His voice is amazing. As it turns out, maybe a little bit too amazing. The lights go down and we hear "Good Evening. My name is…"

And half the crowd says it with him "GEORGE TAKEI!" And now there's laughing, during what is supposed to be a reflection of the theatre season. The video is to get people to concentrate on the nominees. But sections of the crowd are chanting "SU-LU. SU -LU." Nominees, some of whom have waited a lifetime for this moment of recognition, are visibly upset. And so are their moms who flew in from Minnesota or Arkansas and don't know a Klingon from a Romulan.

I don't know if Takei was in attendance, but we invited him. Like Nimoy, he is incredibly gracious and probably was able to chuckle the whole thing away if he was there.

Chapter Four
Mick Foley

Background

Mick Foley and I are both from Long Island. And there the comparisons stop. Foley is a *New York Times* best-selling author for both his autobiography and a children's book. But really, he is a Hall of Fame professional wrestler. He wasn't one of those chiseled physique guys like the Rock. He didn't have the obvious charisma of a Ric Flair or Hulk Hogan. But he was likeable, relatable, funny and self-aware. If you ever see clips of two wrestlers beating each other with baseball bats wrapped in barbed wire or being dropped to a canvas covered in thumbtacks, one is probably Foley. If you ever see the clip of a wrestler being slammed through the top of a steel cage and falling 50 feet and only getting up in a tangled mess with his teeth dislodged from his face, that is definitely Foley. And me, I'm a wrestling fan. That matters for this story. I used to go to matches as a kid.

My first main event was Bruno Sammartino and Gorilla Monsoon against the Executioners, which either means a lot to you, or nothing. I collected idiotic wrestling magazines as a kid that were outdated before

18

they even went to press. And when my friends discarded the practice of being a fan when they realized it frightened away potential dates, I kept up with it. I didn't go to matches or buy magazines. But I watched and enjoyed the TV shows.

Story

You know how even if you're one of those people who really doesn't get star struck, you occasionally just have some moment where you do? I wasn't a huge Mick Foley fan, in awe, desperately waiting to see him. But I did think it was pretty cool that he was coming into a radio station I was running. He was there because he has a long time platonic crush on one of hosts, an adult film actress named Christy Canyon. Christy is every bit the hall of famer in her chosen profession as Mick is in his. I don't think they'd actually met before this day. He mentioned in his autobiography that his wife had agreed to give him "a hall pass" if he should ever be so lucky to meet Christy. Well the book became a best seller and Christy's callers kept asking us on air if there was going to be a rendezvous.

There's one more thing you have to know to make this story work. That is the legend of Bruiser Brody. Brody was a 70's-80's wrestling villain with an unorthodox style, much like Foley. They had hooked up as friends when Foley was breaking in and had a deep mentor/student kind of relationship, along with the friendship.

The details are mysterious and murky, but amidst a feud with another competitor and a promoter in

Puerto Rico, Brody was stabbed to death in the shower. There are a thousand versions of the story, somewhere Brody was murdered and others where he was stabbed in self-defense. The part that matters to these pages is that Foley has often expressed that losing Brody was a devastating, heart wrenching ordeal that he still carries with him.

So we are in the green room, just me and Mick. Foley is jazzed to meet his fantasy dream girl, so much so that he can't sit down. Part of my job is to calm him down and make him feel more comfortable.

What happened next... is so embarrassingly painful for me to recollect that it's one of the few places in this book that I don't remember the exact words I said. But Foley came out with something like, "Jeez I can't believe I'm this nervous. I hope I don't fuck it up."

And I said...

Wait. Before I tell you what I said to Foley. Let me just say, I'm a good husband and a terrific father. Try not to let this moment define your impression of me. I was trying to make small talk. I was trying to build a kinship and let him know I understood him.

And I said...

"Don't worry. No way can it be as bad as Brody getting killed in that shower in Puerto Rico."

Why Foley didn't put me through a wall, I don't know. I can only guess that he was in disbelief.

He simply said, "What? Shut up." And mercifully walked away.

This story does have a happy ending though. I have seen him three times since and he doesn't recognize me at all. That's a good thing.

Lesson

Ask yourself the question, "What is this moment about?" That was a business setting. I don't have to be everybody's best friend. The better play would have been to see if Foley was in a mood to be talkative, or if he needed something. But my mistake wasn't that that I knew too much. It's OK to know as much as you can. But I also know the right way to treat and prep a guest. I chose from the wrong bag of knowledge because I forgot to ask myself what that moment was about.

Footnote

I still watch some wrestling. Usually not around my young daughter because it's... stupid. When my daughter was eight she just happened to walk in while I was watching some match and jumped in front of the TV screaming "I'm *John Cena*!"

I asked her how she knew about the current WWE champ. Turns out one of the boys at school has a "John Cena vs. The Rock" lunch box. Sometimes she'll watch *Monday Night RAW* with me. But she only likes to watch the ring entrances because she is into the fireworks, the music and the fashion statements. The matches and interviews bore her. Unless it's Bayley, a kindhearted hero of modern women's wrestling. She likes Bayley.

Chapter Five
Carol Burnett

Background

Carol was another of our Ovation Award presenters. It was probably in year two or three of the awards, definitely at the old Shubert Theatre in Century City. We had tried to get her in previous years but my best connection was an old friend of mine named John Sokoloff. John was her friend, her personal composer, archivist, house sitter and whatever else she needed, but John really had no vested interest in getting Carol to **my** show. This particular year, Carol had been asked to host by Ted Weiant, one of the theater producers in our group who also happened to know Carol extremely well.

Story

Hopefully, reading even just this far into the book, you have figured out that I like comedy. And let's face it, Carol is not only synonymous with comedy on TV, she is a pioneer. So when I heard that she had arrived backstage, about 20 minutes before we opened the house, I started searching for Ted Weiant, hoping he would introduce me.

On my search for Ted, I went backstage, and just as I opened the big doors that lead down that corridor to the Schubert's dressing rooms, I heard Carol Burnett. Not only that, I could tell from her voice that she was upset. There were three steel doors between me and her, so I could not make out any words, nor could I tell what was getting under her skin.

When I got **two** doors away, I could hear the conversation well enough to make out that the conversation wasn't rude or loud, but Carol seemed to be asking for something that the other party wasn't providing.

When I was just **one** door away, suddenly there was clarity. I heard very clearly what Carol Burnett was saying and the first words I made out were my own name. That's not good. When celebrities are having a beef backstage you really, really, really don't want your name invoked either as the problem or the solution.

As I came through the last door, Carol and one of my team stopped their conversation mid-sentence. "That's him"

"You're Farrell?"

"Yes ma'am"

"Farrell Hirsch?"

"Yes, ma'am. We couldn't be more excited that you are joining us this year. The Los Angeles theater community is…"

"Quiet, Farrell Hirsch"

"…" (That's me being quiet.)

"John Sokoloff says that I'm in good hands with you because you're great. Do something great. "

"Ma'am, greatness can sometimes be achieved in

23

an instant. But it cannot be recognized as such until sufficient time has passed to gain perspective. Abraham Lincoln was considered a tyrant by many contemporaries. A century and a half later he is a giant of history. I submit to you that I am quite likely the Abraham Lincoln of Los Angeles theatre award shows, and if we reconvene in 150 years the greatness that I am doing right here and now will be recognized. Perhaps with a plaque. Perhaps engraved with a depiction of this very meeting between the two of us."

"….." That's Carol being quiet. Until she finally said…. "Now **that** is great."

Lesson

Bullshit has its place. You have to choose your time and place with great care. This could have gone horribly wrong if I misread the situation. But something in her manner—the way she invoked John's name—the challenge. And if you're not good at it **do not attempt**. Because even if you **are** good at it, it still goes off the rails a fairly significant portion of the time.

Chapter Six
Jess Cagle

Background

When I left Playboy, Sirius XM asked me if I was willing to move to New York and run a group of stations for them. That was pretty much a dream job for me. I loved Playboy, that company treated me well and helped me launch a new career, but working there gave people outside the company—sometimes—the impression that you were "the porn guy" or "the sex guy."

So, when SiriusXM offered to bring me to New York and head up a group of stations that had tons of mainstream credibility, I was thrilled. This was going to be my dream job, and that dream was going to start with a big high-profile launch of the new *Entertainment Weekly* station.

Story

I moved to New York in January, leaving my wife behind with my daughter to finish up the school year. They were going to join me over the summer. From almost the first day after I got to SiriusXM, it became apparent that I had either not asked enough questions, or not asked the correct ones, because not very much was as I thought it would be.

I had assumed that the executive who offered me the position, with whom I had worked as a third party entity, was the person to whom I was reporting. I assumed that I would have some staff assigned to me since there were employees out the wazoo and I had several stations to run. But the really damaging assumptions were those that concerned *Entertainment Weekly*. When I arrived in New York I was told that, officially, the *EW* folks had to approve me, but that the ball was in motion and a meeting was set up as a formality. And I had assumed that much like my relationship with Playboy, *they* were the brand experts who would tell me how they saw *EW*, and my job would be to turn that into radio genius.

None of those assumptions were correct. The meeting we had was really a job interview within the job I already moved across country to perform. And it did not go well, because of that final assumption. I was very eager to hear what they had to say about *EW*; it was an incredible brand, a career-changing opportunity, and a bridge between SiriusXM and Time Warner—and a nice place to be.

I met with Editor in Chief Jess Cagle—who you will recognize on the Oscar's red carpet coverage for ABC, and another *EW* bigwig. Typical midtown fancy lunch meeting. I think I had a lobster sandwich as we played a most regrettable game of verbal ping-pong.

"So guys, tell me about your vision, is there a mission statement for the magazine or the radio station?"

And they answered, "We really want to hear **your** vision" Of course they did, it was a job interview. But I didn't know that.

"I've read the last six issues, and I have tons of ideas. But the best way to move forward is to avoid the false starts. Tell me where you see this going, ideally, and I can come back in a few days with a brilliant roadmap."

And, obviously, it looked to them that I was avoiding answers because I was either unprepared, or without any substance. To their credit, they tried a different tact.

"We're very based in columns and features, which ones do you think would translate well."

That was a fair, smart question. My answer was neither.

"Guys, we have to think big picture before we get lost in the details"

There was no way, with those horrid answers, that they were going to let me run their station. And I got the word within a day or so that they talked to the President of SiriusXM and asked for someone else.

Lesson

Well, there are tons of them. First, please note that I was very clear in this story that the mistakes were my mistakes. My incorrect assumptions didn't come from anyone lying to me, or intentionally misleading me. I just thought I had it all figured out... and so I stopped asking important and relevant questions.

My other failure, ironically, was something at which I'm usually pretty good. I didn't read that room, that conversation or those men at all. I should have picked up on what they were asking and why. All the pieces of the puzzle were in my head and I never put them together. In most cases I think of myself as a terrific improviser, and that skill has helped me at a thousand business meetings. But, painfully, I didn't access that skill on *EW* day. I actually had a notebook full of amazing ideas—complete with illustrations—that I immodestly say would have made the launch of that station even better than it eventually was.

But I didn't give myself the chance.

When my boss came to tell me that the *EW* guys didn't approve me, I was stunned. Remember, I wasn't even really conscious of there being an approval process. He said he didn't know why they rejected me, and I certainly didn't. But he did tell me a story about a job he had lost as a younger man, and how it haunted him. He said it took him many years to figure out what he had done wrong. For me... it only took about three years.

Addendum

While my time working in SiriusXM's New York City office wasn't even remotely successful, one thing I always enjoyed was that as I was leaving for the evening, at least once per week, there would be an incredibly cool celebrity performing in the fishbowl studio. One day on the way out I stopped in for half of a live Tony Bennett concert. Another day I paused in the lobby as Al Gore was taking off the cuff questions from listeners.

There was a pretty good rule about us not bothering guests for photos. But the one time I could not resist was when the stars of a Disney show called *Austin and Ally* were visiting. My daughter's favorite show. That photo is my only keepsake from my time there.

Chapter Seven
Pitbull

Background

Lil Jon is the King of Crunk. On the one hand, that is really all you need to know. On the other hand… the average "guy like me" is not likely to have a great working knowledge of crunk royalty. Many can't tell the Duke of West Crunkfalia from the actual King.

Crunk is almost like music in some ways. People go to performances, or dance to it in clubs. Some even download audio files containing Crunk.

Lil Jon was the first to break out of Atlanta's Crunk scene the way (and this is for those "guys like me") Nirvana came out of Seattle's grunge scene, or the Beatles came from Liverpool to start the British invasion. But unlike those others, Lil Jon was as much a producer and entrepreneur as an artist. And so he attempted to lift the entire Atlanta Crunk scene with him.

Story

It all started at the most spectacular party I have ever attended. It was Playboy's Super Bowl party in Miami, and Lil Jon was "spinning" that night and dubbed the official "host" of the party. Attention "guys like me!" He was **not** riding an exercise bicycle really, really fast, his spinning means he was DJing the party.

The event was held at Miami's American Airlines Arena. Yes, the entire arena! The floor which normally housed an NBA team became a giant dance floor. There was an ice cream truck driving around inside. There was an insane Sushi station. Lots of celebrities and athletes. And literally thousands of incredibly beautiful, entirely unattached, party-enhancing, brand-invigorating young women.

My job that night was to supervise the red carpet crew, which essentially was just Miss August 2004 Pilar Lastra, as she interviewed whoever came down the red carpet. We were Playboy Radio, and this was a… no, it was *the* Playboy party. So there was no gotcha journalism and no embarrassing questions. The red carpet ran long, the weather turned cold, and Pilar was needed inside to perform other duties. But many of our biggest names had not yet arrived. So guess who was left to do interviews… me.

I was OK with retired ball players like Joe Girardi and Warren Moon, and even some corporate CEO types. But now I get a message from our PR team that our host for the evening has arrived and we have to capture him for radio. If you want to get a sense of how well I did, look back at the phrase, "guys like me." Now, here is the transcript of how I opened the interview. Read it out loud, wherever you are right now, read it out loud, in the voice of that "guy like me." You won't get more than six words in before you're embarrassed for me. Maybe… it will only take a single syllable.

I actually said the words, "Yo yo, King of the Crunk in da House!"

Right. Lightning *should* have come from the clear skies, stuck me on the temple, and ended this. No such luck.

Lil Jon answered, "Hey."

So I continued, "The man of the hour, Lil Jon, host of tonight's Playboy SuperBowl Party, what are you expecting to see inside?"

Lil Jon, "Man I'm up on stage, lights in the eyes. I probably won't be able to see shit."

Me, "That's cool." In retrospect I cannot fathom what about it might be cool, or for that matter, why I bothered continuing, "And there's more news in Crunkland, word is you have an album dropping next week"

If you are **not** a "guy like me," you are wondering what the hell was wrong with me. If you **are** a "guy like me," you're still wondering, but it comes out as "Oy Gevalt."

A few hours later, in another part of the arena, I ran into Lil Jon in a milieu where I was much more at home. The urinal line in the men's room of a sports arena. Lil Jon sees me, laughs and shakes his head in pity. "What the fuck, man?"

"Yeah, sorry, I'm not on air talent. I run the station, but I lost my playmate host before you showed up, so…"

This one is a direct quote. "You no on-air talent and you no off-air talent…" which was **more** insulting because my penis was already out to urinate.

We talked for about another 10 minutes and then exchanged contact info… in the men's room… of the Playboy party.

Several months later, I noticed Lil Jon was swinging through LA doing appearances promoting something (Yo yo, maybe that album finally dropped?). So like a jackass radio guy, I called to try and talk him into coming on the station. He didn't want to. But he offered me a deal. He had a new artist he was promoting who wasn't getting any airplay yet. He wanted me to take this guy as a guest.

Why would I want a guest with no resume?

"This guy is gonna be big." I just took that as appropriate hyperbole. "Take him, you got me next time I'm in town"

"I have your word on that?" I was attempting to maneuver him into a verbal contract because obviously that was entirely enforceable.

And that is how I became the first person to book Pitbull on a radio show.

Lesson

From your worst screw up, often come the seeds of greatness. Had I been too embarrassed of my performance on that red carpet, I might never have called John.

And I had every right to be embarrassed. Not only because I was terrible, but because our morning show played the clip of me being terrible about once per week for three years. Millions of audience members knew me only as that fumbling inappropriate red carpet buffoon.

So don't let failure derail your success train. Laugh it off and turn it into something useful.

Addendum

Same kinda story, with a different outcome. I played softball with the same group of guys in Beverly Hills every Sunday morning for about 15 years. One day our centerfielder, an attorney named Kenny Dusick, asked if I would do him a favor. He said his son was a drummer and had formed a band with his schoolmates. He was wondering if I could play them on my stations.

It was all very cordial, but I had to explain why I couldn't just play any song handed to me by a friend. I had a certain obligation to the audience. We had millions of listeners and a system in place, and royalty rights that had to be paid. I had hosts that were begging me to get "real" bands into studio, so I can't just throw this particular favor around.

And he understood.

But that is the story about how I was **not** the first guy to book Maroon 5 on a radio show.

Chapter Eight
Bill Cosby

Background

For a least a quarter of a century I had been a step or two away from the perimeter of Bill Cosby's world. While I was still in college, two of my high school friends went to work on *The Cosby Show*. And so I had always heard stories about what was going on there. Later I had worked on a documentary Mr. Cosby voiced. And over the years I just seemed to befriend lots of people who knew, or worked with him.

Now before we go any further, I have to put out of your mind the idea that there was ever any discussion of alleged sexual impropriety. Not a whisper, not an off color joke. Nothing. At the time of this event, none of that was known to me, or the general public.

Story

Cosby had an amazingly varied career. Standup comedy, TV cop shows, hit movies, legendary sitcoms. But this story was about his 25-year run as host/emcee of the Playboy Jazz Festival. Even though his only duties were to introduce an act for 30 seconds, once every hour, Mr. Cosby did not like to be disturbed during the Jazz Festival. And even though there was plenty of time and availability, Mr. Cosby hated to be disturbed on the day of the Jazz Festival's Press Conference. In general, Mr. Cosby did not like to be disturbed and he found pretty much everything to be a disturbance.

But our job was to arrange a 15-minute recording session with him to help promote the festival on our station. He considered Mr. Hefner a close friend and acquiesced when the request came directly from Hef. With a condition. He would not come to our studio, and did not want to allow us in his home. So he agreed to meet us up at the Playboy mansion for a maximum of 20 minutes.

While we were setting up in the back part of the foyer which has a giant window overlooking the pool, Cosby must have mentioned a half a dozen times that we should either hurry up, get our act together, or just generally act in a more professional manner. He also had little interest in the script we had written. He wanted us to just feed him the times and dates of the event he was promoting and he felt comfortable improvising the rest.

Although we agreed to every single request, he remained surly. It's the only time I've met him, so I assume it was a bad day. But he was just not in a cooperative mood. He kept getting the dates of the event wrong, and demanding we fix it with an edit. It was my job to explain that we couldn't edit in the correct dates until we had him speaking the correct dates. But my explanation was interrupted by a long loud screech that sounded like a heavy lawn chair having its metal legs dragged along a cement patio.

We all turned to look through those giant windows that faced the pool. Cosby unleashed a barrage of anger at us for not controlling the sound in our environment and letting something so hideous interrupt comedic genius. There was lots of cursing, things like "Somebody stop that stupid motherfucker from whatever the fuck he is fucking doing to fuck up my fucking…" And then Cosby sees that it is Hef dragging the metal legs of the lounge chair across the cement. Boom! One hundred eighty degrees.

Cosby was instantly transformed into a kitten, thanking Hef for letting us use the house and *apologized* if he was disturbing Mr. Hefner's "work" It was all laughs and giggles. Clearly we were done for the day.

Lesson

There's always a bigger dog on the yard.

Also, though it isn't the lesson for this chapter, in fairness to Cosby I need to mention that we were told later that a large part of his consternation was due to his failing eyesight. He had no choice but to improvise if he couldn't read a script. And he had no choice but to participate, since it was a direct request from Hef.

Addendum

One of the improv pieces that Mr. Cosby did that day involves inviting a pretty young lady to the Jazz

Festival and plying her with drinks so she can relax and enjoy herself. This was years before the drugging and rape charges against Crosby, so we never gave it any attention. But years later, my producer for the day was listening through the old files and heard this very peculiar audio clip. Maybe this was foreshadowing the sordid allegations; maybe it was his attempt to embrace party culture, to be edgy and set contrast to the lovable Cliff Huxtable. Context changes the meaning of those bits; something relatively benign becomes... not.

Chapter Nine
Bruce Springsteen

Background

I am far from alone among men of my generation in elevating Bruce Springsteen to the position of exalted Rock God/Deified Social Commentator/Voice of the Disenfranchised/Greatest Living Frontman/Humble Artistic Genius etc.

It was his song "Thunder road" that we all used to play on our car 8-tracks before heading out to cause the kind of damage we were hardly capable of causing. Why we so strongly identified with his characters who needed to work in the fields 'til they got their backs burned, and facts learned. I can tell you. Most of my friends didn't ride mansions of glory and suicide machines. They drove new sports cars that carried them to post graduate degrees at Ivy League schools. But he captured that whole teenage boy hormone fueled rage—that co-existence of ultimate hope and despair, and sex, and cars, and guitars, and sex.

But I cannot imagine who would have been more jaw dropping to run into, than the Boss. Belushi was dead. Woody Allen was in New York. Lech Wałęsa was in Poland.

Story

We were going to see a movie one afternoon in 1988 or 89. Why? For the same reason everyone in Los Angeles goes to see a movie on a weekday afternoon. We had booked a freelance writing assignment and the deadline was more than a day away. So we went to the movies.

I don't remember at all what film we saw. I remember that it was playing at the Century City Mall, and that there were about four sets of escalators between the theatre and where we had parked. I wish I could tell you what movie it was, whether we liked it, what we were talking about… Or anything else. But my brain was about to be shaken like an Etch a Sketch and reset to blank.

My buddy and I went down the first escalator. That's where we validated our parking. Then the second escalator. Then about halfway down the third I noticed a couple heading up. I made eye contact with the guy and he nodded a blank hello, and I returned it. No big deal. Except that I kept thinking he looked familiar. But who the heck was he? Someone from the gym? An actor I had auditioned for something? My buddy hadn't seen him and was trying to help me out, "Did he look like anyone famous?"

"Yeah, he looked a little like… holy crap. That was Bruce Springsteen!"

"No."

"Yes."

"No."

"Yes."

"No way."

"I'm pretty sure."

"It can't be Bruce."

"I think it was."

So we get to the next landing and turn around and head back up the escalators. Mostly so my buddy can prove me wrong. And, let's face it, I probably was wrong.

When we got to the top of the escalators we were back in the mall, maybe 30 yards from the ticket window. And we spot the couple. They're on line to the very same theatre we just came out of. So we got on line right in back of them.

Remember when I said we had a writing gig that wasn't due yet. It was very much an early career assignment... or, in other words, there wasn't any advance money and there was no way we could afford both another movie *and* the extra three hours of parking fees.

But we were on line behind possible Mr. and Mrs. Springsteen. And we kept trying to peek around the corners of his head to get a glimpse. And we were trying to share information in a whispered code as to not embarrass this person we were stalking and staring at. It didn't take long before he knew exactly what we were doing. Maybe it wasn't his first day out in public as a famous guy.

He turned around and said, "What are you guys seeing?"

We were writing partners and both came up with the same brilliant improvised line, "I don't know."

He told us what he was seeing and said he heard it was pretty good.

I'm an idiot and said, "It is. We just saw it a few minutes ago."

He laughed that strange awkwardly sincere two syllable Bruce-laugh you see on interviews, got his tickets and went off into the theatre.

We waited 'til he was out of sight and started jumping around like we just actually got paid for that freelance writing job.

Lesson

What were Springsteen's options as we breathed our over-aged fanboy breath on the back of his neck? He could have ignored us. But that might have kept us in pursuit. He could have said, "Look, guys, I'm out with my wife. Can you give me some space?" But that might have made him seem conceited. So what did he do? He chose to treat us like equals, like peers, like humans. He treated us as though he was just some guy on a movie line, and we were just some schmoes behind him. And so that was what we instantly became. Had he considered us stalkers, or a nuisance, or a burden, we would have become those things. Treating us like regular guys was so disarming and so charming that we were completely taken aback… in such a terrific way.

Addendum

I can only think of one other cool singer story.

I was in New York on business and staying at one of my favorite hotels, the Le Parker Meridien. On my second day there I was taking a late-night elevator ride up to my floor when who should get on, but Tom Jones.

Yeah, the Welsh singer, *Sir* Tom Jones.

He and the guy I took to be his manager were quite taken by the television above the sliding doors. As we climbed upward, we all stared at a Tom and Jerry cartoon. As the doors opened, Jones turned to me and said, "Do all the hotels have TV's in the elevators now?"

And, being me, I had said, "It's not unusual."

He looked disgusted and left.

Chapter Ten
Stiller and Meara,
with Ben Stiller and Gwyneth Paltrow

Background

I loved Stiller and Meara. They were my favorite comedy team. More than Nicols and May, or Abbot and Costello. That would be Jerry Stiller, who you probably know better from *King of Queens*, or as George's father on *Seinfeld*. And that would be Anne Meara, who was series regular on everything from *The Dick Van Dyke Show* to *Sex in the City* and *All My Children*, to *Alf*. So, I hired them to be presenters at The Ovation Awards one year even though you couldn't really say they were best known for legit stage work.

Story

Jerry Stiller called me every other day leading up to the awards show. And it was very much like talking to Frank Costanza. Read this out loud in his nasal, high-velocity Brooklyn near-shout to get the full effect. "Farrell, it's Jerry. When is that thing again? Monday night?"

And then two days later, "Farrell, it's Jerry. I know you said it was the Schubert Theatre. I wrote that down, but it's the one in Los Angeles, right? They have them all over the place. Like Burger Kings."

And then the next day "Farrell, it's Jerry. I know you said you couldn't provide a car service. But if I drive myself is there somewhere to park? You can go that far, can't you? A parking spot?"

From someone else it might have been a pain in my ass. But each of those opening statements led to really warm and wonderful conversations. For a week in the mid 90's Jerry Stiller and I were chatting regularly about our lives, like friends.

Then comes the day of the show. "Farrell, it's Jerry. I need a favor. "

I'm in my tuxedo, ready to leave for the theatre. The show starts in about two hours. "What do you need Jerry?"

"I need two more tickets"

"I don't think there are any. I know we are completely sold out."

"It's for my son. It's not every day you can be there when your parents get an award."

"Jerry, you guys are *presenting* an award, not receiving one."

"No, his girlfriend's mother is nominated for something or other."

"Its two hours before the show. The whole seating plan is finished and…"

"The kid wants to be a director. I want him to meet you, schmooze a little, maybe you can help him out and introduce him around."

Like I have nothing else to do tonight.

"I'll tell you what. Have him come to the box office and ask for me and I'll see what I can do. Maybe I can sneak him into the back of the house."

"You are a freaking angel."

What the hell was I supposed to do with this guy's freeloading son? By the time I arrived at the theatre, my mind was elsewhere. Mariette Hartley didn't like who she was presenting with, Ed Begley Jr. wanted to talk about growing up in the same hometown as me. Jerry's kid was not in the forefront of my thoughts.

But about ten minutes before show time, someone from the box office comes running to me, "Oh my God, oh my God, oh my God, oh my God, oh my God."

"What?"

"Gwyneth Paltrow is at the ticket window"

"Really? That's cool. Good for her for supporting theatre."

"No. She's asking for **you**!"

"Me? I don't know her. Why would she ask for me?"

"She said her boyfriend is parking the car and you were going to leave tickets for him"

"Nobody I know is, or could ever be, dating Gwyneth Paltrow. Are you fucking with me?"

"Do you ever read a paper? Her boyfriend is Ben Stiller!"

"I don't know Ben Stiller. He's a big movie star. The closest thing I know is…. Shit…. Jerry Stiller's son who wants to be a director is *Ben Stiller* (the hugely successful actor and director), and his girlfriend is Gwyneth Paltrow, whose mother Blythe Danner, is accepting a humanitarian award tonight! **Aah!**"

Needless to say, we found them seats. Very good seats.

But I did ask Jerry after the show… "Why didn't you just tell me it was Ben and Gwyneth?"

"I didn't want to be a pest"

Lesson

Ask more questions. Stop and think about the whole situation. There are a thousand permutations of the possibilities and when you rush through just trying to get to the **next** task, you shortchange the current one.

I am still guilty of this sin quite often. There is something in my nature that always has me trying to propel myself a few levels into the future before I fix the present. Even in writing this book. I wrote a first draft… and then never got around to proofreading or editing for months because I was on to the next thing.

Try to remember a line from Charles Emerson Winchester's first episode of *M*A*S*H*. "I do one thing at a time. I do it very well. And then I move on"

Addendum

Stiller and Meara's performance on stage that night was one of my favorites of all time. They started by thanking me for writing them something, and then said they were going to ignore it. So they crumpled it up and threw the script page across to the far side of the stage.

Then they improvised a piece about how The Ovation Awards was really the "Ovulation Awards, and are given out every 28 days" and so on and so on… joke after joke. They had a punch line/exit line planned for when a joke bombed. But everything they said made the crowd roar louder.

They were hysterical. The two-minute bit went on for almost ten.

And when a line finally fell flat, they looked at each other in a panic, and used their planned exit… They crawled across the stage to pick up the crumpled script they had discard, apologizing to me along the way.

Brilliant.

Chapter Eleven
Annette Bening

Background

Have you ever heard a celebrity complain about being a celebrity? The lack of privacy, or the constant public pressure, or how the mean-spirited press reports can overwhelm them. It's just a part of the job, right? It goes with the territory, right? And it gives them license to be an ass once in a while, right?

Well then why doesn't any of that apply to Annette Bening? She has a hugely successful career, Oscars, Golden Globes, etc. But you never see crazy stories about her, even in the worst of the gossip rags. I am here to expose her deep dark secret. She made a pact with the devil. And in this pact, she gets immunity from paparazzi and tabloids, and in exchange she has to be the single most gracious human on earth. In my experience, she has lived up to her end of the deal.

Story

We asked Annette Bening to be a presenter at The Ovation Awards in the same year she was nominated for an award. She would be presenting the award for "Best Play." A high profile category. She was nominated in the "Best Actress in a Play" category for her work in *Hedda Gabler* at the Geffen Playhouse. Also nominated in that category were Faye Dunaway for *Master Class*—a one-woman show about opera star Maria Callas. Oh, and Carol Burnett for Sondheim's *Company.* So there you have it. The four nominees were Annette Bening, Faye Dunaway, Carol Burnett and Tracey Middendorf. You don't recognize that last name? That's part of the point here.

When Ms. Bening showed up we realized that she was incredibly beautiful, incredibly charming, and incredibly pregnant. From her appearance I would guess she was in about her 16th month. As I mentioned before, those of us working in the Los Angeles theatre community have a double inferiority complex. Always playing second fiddle to New York in theatre. Always playing second fiddle to movies and TV in L.A. And so we were deeply moved that not only did she agree to present, but to do so when her water might break at any minute.

When the presenter in the Best Actress category ran through the list of nominees, Annette was in the wings waiting to go on stage either right now as a winner, or in three minutes as a presenter for the next category. Carol Burnett was in the audience. Faye Dunaway was on tour with that same show but had sent a video we could play in the event that she won.

And the Ovation Award for Best Actress goes to… Tracey Middendorf!

A theater stage is a great equalizer, and there is no reason the more famous, more accoladed actress must be better than the relatively unknown actress. And on this night our collective voting body screamed that out quite loudly. And every artist, from every theatrical discipline, who had *ever* felt like the underdog during their career rose in unison to their feet and cried.

But no one cried and crumpled and was resurrected with more pride, all in a single three second span, than our hero, Tracey Middendorf. Her acceptance speech was glorious and gracious. It was clear she was "unfamous," but not unschooled. This is a career actress of astounding merit—which very simply does not always equate to fame. Now I want to be fair, and Tracey had done *Beverly Hills 90210* and some other shows. But she wasn't a star.

Her speech was full of the usual thank you's, and well… you know how winners always say how they are "honored just to be nominated in a group of artists for whom I have such unfettered admiration?" She was sincerely dumbfounded and almost embarrassed. You get the feeling that she thought it was one of the Steve Harvey moments and the PA was about to announce, "We have a correction to announce."

As she walked off with her glowing green statue, she passed Annette Bening in the wings. Their eyes met, and I am told Tracey mouthed something like, "I'm sorry." Annette would have none of it. She grabbed Tracey's arm, and as V.O. announcer said, "Ladies and Gentlemen, Annette Bening…" Annette went to the mic and said "And I will be presenting tonight with my colleague, Tracey Middendorf"

Standing freakin Ovation.

Eight months pregnant and a minute after losing a

prestigious award, nobody is obligated to open their heart in that way. But to make the effort to say, "No, really, you *are* one of us and you *deserve* this." Wow.

Lesson

The lesson here is that grace costs you nothing, but earns you everything. Both ladies have become indelibly etched into the memories of those of us who attended that evening.

Addendum

This story was more beyond the realm of comprehension when it happened, than it would seem now. Check Tracey's *IMDB* page now and you can see she has gone on to a really nice career in both TV and film. She's been a regular on *Boardwalk Empire, Scream, 24,* and *The Last Ship.*

I still get excited about seeing her name in the credits of a show.

Chapter Twelve
Kenny G

Background

One of the first things my writing partner and I did when we arrived in Los Angeles in 1987 to write movies and TV shows, was find ways to avoid writing movies and TV shows. Our diversions included writing questions for a new board game, spending a day driving modified golf carts on busy freeways, and hanging around the sets of music videos where we knew people and thought we might get paid... to do something... eventually.

Our favorite company was Gorilla Films. We never really knew who owned, financed or controlled the company. But the director, Rick, was our much more accomplished buddy. And the two producers seemed pretty good at getting gigs. Well, at least better than us. We didn't have one.

Story

Kenny G was at the top of his game in 1987-88, and his new single "Against Doctor's Orders" was expected to be another hit. So the record company was willing to front an unusually high budget for this music video. The concept was that Kenny was kind of a Pied Piper character that runs through a hospital playing his mini-saxophone… whatever he plays, I knew what he played back then.… and his music brings people to life. In a time when everything was hokey, this video stood out. But that was semi-intentional. Nobody was trying to make cinema. We just wanted viewers to have fun. And littered through the hospital were cameos by the wildly and slightly famous. Dudley Moore, an A-List comic actor played a doctor. Scott Baio was a cadaver. His girlfriend at the time, Nicollette Sheridan, played a nurse. One hit-wonder Robbie Neville was in there somewhere, as was VH1 Original VJ (and it mattered a lot in 1988) Roger Rose. Character actor Michael J. Pollard was an orderly.

My writing partner and I make a cameo as two guys in lab coats walking in the background. That will matter as the story unfolds.

Though I had no official title, or duties, or salary on this project, Eric and I were promised some kind of producer titles. That's a nice first credit at 24. So I called back to my Mom in New York and told her everything I just told you.

"Mom, I just helped produce a music video" (an exaggeration).

"That's nice" She wasn't as excited as I thought she would be.

"It was for Kenny G, the Saxophone player" See?!?! I told you I knew back then.

"He's still around?"

"Still around? He just started his career. And Dudley Moore was in it, from *Arthu*r!"

"I heard he's a drunk"

"That was the movie. I have no idea about real life but Scott Baio is in it too"

"What's the matter? Was Fonzie too busy?"

"OK, I get it, I'm sending you a VHS. At about 2:24, Eric and I pop out of a door for like a second"

"Why didn't you say you were in it? When is it going to be on TV? I have to tell your grandmother. Have you told her about this? Don't tell her. She won't understand? That is so wonderful, you're starring in a movie!"

Lesson

People need to *see* it, to get it. Hollywood jobs like directing and producing sound so amorphous to the rest of the world. I don't think they really understand the job titles. But to actually see someone you know on that screen. Even if it's just the back of their heads and they're silent, is a validation that they've made it.

The lesson here is that if you want people to understand the value of an experience or an event, you need to give them something tangible. Something they can see or touch.

I haven't told my mother yet that I have written this book. It won't mean anything to her until she holds an actual copy in her hands.

I saw Kenny G several million years later, in 2010. I said,"You won't remember but I worked on a music video you did." And he said "Against Doctors Orders, right?"

That sucker remembered. Good for him.

Chapter Thirteen
Michael Eisner

Background

There are three things you need to know for the background of this story.

One, there was a time when Mike Eisner ran show business. He was the living symbol of a benevolent power broker. He ran Disney, which owned ABC, which owned ESPN. He would appear in promotional videos with Mickey Mouse and get top billing. At the time they also owned the NHL team named after one of their popular kid's films, The Mighty Ducks of Anaheim.

Two, I had a job working with the coaching staff of the Mighty Ducks of Anaheim. I was part of a team that kept stats in the press box and relayed them to the coaching staff, so they could make more informed strategic decisions.

Three, I had a wealthy uncle who had all his suits and sport coats hand made by a personal tailor in Hong Kong. As absurd as it might sound that someone might fly to Asia to get fitted, guys with that kind of money have done much weirder things with it. It would seem unlikely that these three disparate facts would come together to make a story. And yet...

Story

I was working in the arena press box on the very top level of the building that was then called "The Pond" to keep in step with the Ducks theme. Where do Ducks play? On a pond? In this case, a frozen pond. The Ducks even had a theme song they played during every pre-game ritual called "Rock the Pond" where they likened their team to a "surge of force that never dies." The claims to a renewable energy source aside, "Rock The Pond" got played each game as the team's costumed mascot, WildWing, was lowered from the rafters to the ice, so that he could skate through a burning ring of fire.

The man inside the suit had only been hired for his skating skills, not his ability to stay calm while dangling from a strap a few hundred feet above the crowd. On a good day, he was skittish. But then came a bad day. As they were lowering WildWing to the ice, the gurney malfunctioned with WildWing swinging way above the ice, and about five thousand kids in the arena were either horrified or anticipating a new kind of show. Dangling up there he was just about eye level with those of us in the press box. And even through the suit and giant mascot head, you could see a person fearing for their life.

By happenstance, Disney CEO Michael Eisner was in the press box that day. That wasn't unprecedented, but it was somewhat unusual. You never want to be the guy in charge of a botched operation on the day the boss pays a visit, but you *really*, don't want to be the Disney employee who plunged a beloved mascot to his death in front of Eisner.

It took a good 20 harrowing minutes, but they finally found a way to get WildWing down safely. As the tension dissipated, Eisner turned and looked right at me. Those of us who were lowly stat boys knew to stay out of his path. Not that he was ever anything but pleasant, it's just that he was so many rungs above us on this ladder that the respectful thing to do was steer clear. But then he stepped right into my path as though he wanted to tell me something. But instead he rubbed the outer edge of my lapel between his right thumb and forefinger. I was wearing one of the sport coats my uncle tired of—Herringbone. Probably hadn't been worn more than ten times in its life. I could tell by Eisner's expression he was both impressed and confused as to why the lowest guy on the totem pole had a coat of this quality.

From that day forward, and for the next two seasons while I worked there, Mr. Eisner greeted me by name, and with a handshake.

Lesson

Truth be told, if jacket and tie weren't mandatory in a working pressbox, I would have been in jeans and sneakers. I am very much not the kind of person who judges myself, or others, by their clothes. But this lesson is for all of you who think like me. Even if you don't judge people by their apparel. Everyone else does. And while good enough is good enough to get by. Go the extra mile if you want your career to go the extra mile.

Footnote

Getting stuck swinging from the rafters was only WildWing's second worst day. There was another incident where, while jumping through the fiery hoop, WildWing's tail caught on fire. The crowd was screaming and pointing… WildWing was just waiving back at them, thankful for the attention.

You can't really see very much in those mascot suits. But you can smell. Especially the toxic burning fumes of a melting cartoon duck. I have cherished visual memories of firefighters sliding across the ice trying to spray flame retardant foam up the duck's ass.

Chapter Fourteen
Jenna Jameson

BackStory

During the years I worked for Playboy, they purchased the Jenna Jameson empire from Jenna and her then-husband, Jay Grdina. I don't remember how much they paid, but it was astoundingly high. At least enough so that we were all floored by the number when we heard it.

I can remember that my first thought was "Wow, I can't imagine what asset would depreciate faster than an 'already peaked' porn star." But all the Harvard MBA guys told me that I didn't understand the value of the internet library, and the subscription model that Club Jenna had perfected. This was the future of, not just porn, not just entertainment, but all of business.

History will not be kind to those who proclaimed to have seen in to the future that day. But OK, they took their shot based on what they believed. And if nothing else, they had the library of the biggest name in their industry, a budding crossover star, and a delightfully charming young lady.

Story

It was explained to me by my boss that some clause in that deal made it mandatory for Jenna to do a certain amount of days of publicity for her brand, to help Playboy maximize its potential. There had been some attempts to get her to some other things before I stepped up. Some she didn't accept. Some she apparently just no-showed. Others just did not go as smoothly as planned.

But I knew she could be an asset to Playboy Radio. The folks at Sirius would be impressed by the name, and all we had to do was get some decent content from her.

My best Jenna story from those days is about the segment we created for her on the radio. But there isn't a way to tell that story without using a vile word that makes me uncomfortable, and telling how Jenna applied it to two public figures, Chelsea Handler and our CEO Christie Hefner.

My second best Jenna story from those days ends with someone throwing a punch at me on a train from Wrigley Field to downtown Chicago because I invoked her name. If that person didn't want to be associated with her in a private conversation, they undoubtedly would rather not be associated with her in this book. To be fair, that person has sworn to me that it was just a joke and they never meant to make contact with my head and their fist. I'm not so sure.

My third best Jenna story involves setting up a dinner meeting between Jenna and my staff, at an ever-changing series of restaurants depending upon where the best paparazzi might be on this particular evening. The final results of that evening fall under a confidentiality agreement I signed. But hypothetically, if one party demands to make the reservations as to *avoid* photographers, and then seats themselves in the best seat to be shot by the photographers, and they shows up *before* she does... I don't know.

Lesson

If all the little stories of your life have sad endings, then most likely so will the larger story of your life. I can't say I ever knew Jenna particularly well. But I can say there have always been stories that she didn't treat anyone in her circle particularly well, and that includes herself.

And who knows, there might yet be a happily ever after for her. I have heard in the past year she found a new religion, got married, and has just had a baby girl..

I hope she is well. She has suffered enough and deserves to be happy.

Footnote

So, about five years after all of those above stories, our paths crossed again and... there isn't a single detail about that story that I can divulge.

Chapter Fifteen
Nathan Lane

Background

I'm not sure how it happened, but there was this one
year we actually scored Nathan Lane to be the host of
The Ovation Awards. He was the perfect candidate in
that he was a legit Broadway star, he was very well
known in the mainstream of entertainment, and best of
all, clearly a hugely talented host. I booked most of the
presenters that year, but not Mr. Lane. I had no
connection to him. But I was responsible once again
for writing the script, such as it was—the inane cringe-
inducing little patter that is mandatory before
announcing a winner.

Story

There is only one rehearsal for an awards show like
this. It has to happen when the theatre is dark. And so,
the night before the event we met Mr. Lane for the
first time. He was running late and not necessarily in
the best of moods. Or perhaps it was my fault for not
exchanging some pleasantries before jumping directly
into business and asking if he had received the script.

He said he had, but that he hadn't read it because he decided "just to hire a real professional to write one."

That sure felt like a shot at me… at the time.

We moved on to a blocking rehearsal where he was pretty resistant to stage directions that we had prepared… and designed lighting for.

And that sure felt like a shot… at the time.

And about half way through he asked for a break, walked out the back door of the theatre, and didn't return for the rest of the evening. Remember, this was the only chance *any* of us had to rehearse.

I called his management and they assured me he would be there the following evening in good spirits and blow the roof off the place. I had little faith. I also had little recourse. We had sold more tickets than ever before and it was at least in part due to his name.

The following evening Nathan Lane showed up on time, I can't really tell you his mood because I was in a crappy one and stayed away. But I snuck into the back of the house in time to hear, "Ladies and Gentleman, Nathan Lane," followed by a standing ovation. I learned during that day, that the "real writer" who Lane brought in was Bruce Vilanch. Asking Bruce Vilanch to script your awards show is like asking Sinatra to sing you "Happy Birthday." The best of the best of the all-time freakin' best. And he did in his opening monologue the one thing I would never do, the one thing destined to cause audience revolt. A good portion of the monologue was a devastating put down of the very Los Angeles theatre community we had gathered to celebrate—in which the entire audience made both their art and their living. And they *loved it*!!!!!

I knew instantly that this was *much* funnier than what I had written for Lane, and much better suited to Lane himself. And if I hadn't known, the audience response would have informed me quite clearly. Oh, and I also knew that the evening's program listed me as the writer, so I would still get the credit.

Every single one of my peers was in the crowd that night, and every single one of them congratulated me for "nailing it" and for being courageous enough not to be scared of collective self-deprecation. I told as many people as possible the story about how my work was usurped and bettered by Vilanch and Lane's cabal. And I tried my best to say it in a way that wasn't bitterly driven by ego. Though I probably didn't hide the fact that I was hurt, not by them stealing my limelight, but by the proof that they were right to do it.

Lesson

I'm a good writer. I have skills that have allowed me to make a career out of crafting words for a few decades. And there have been some projects where I thought my work was actually better than good. Ok, maybe not everyone shared that opinion, but I like me.

But into every life comes someone who is just better than you at a skill you embrace. Despite how much I wanted it, I was never the best hockey player on my team. I was never the best dancer on the floor. So as an adult, I really didn't want anyone to prove they could write something better than I could. Too bad. There's always going to be someone better than you and there are times when, for the greater good, you have to graciously step aside and acknowledge greatness.

Addendum

Sometimes later, two of my favorite theatre producers were involved in a musical revue with a script by Bruce Vilanch. I read the script and didn't like it. And I was happy to share my opinion with my producer friends.

And I was happy to subtly hint that I could do better.

And then not so subtly.

And then openly campaign for them to fire Vilanch (which I'm sure in retrospect was as impossible as it was imprudent) and hire me.

And then volunteer to write a new show for free, just to usurp Bruce Vilanch.

Well… my friends were nice enough to humor me.

Of course in the middle of this I get a call from my father, "Did you ever hear of a guy named Bruce Vilanch?"

Bruce's mother was in a nursing home in Florida where my father's wife was working and they thought maybe we would like to meet because, as my father said, "They tell me he is a very good writer, maybe you could learn something?"

Chapter Sixteen
Danny Glover and Rita Moreno

Background

Another one from the annals of The Ovation Awards.

When you put together an awards show, the pairing of presenters is a challenging art form. You might chose to pair together people who share a common history. You might choose to pair them by theme. Or you might just go by some hunch of eclectic nuance and say to yourself, "I just *have* to see these two people together."

Story

And so one year we paired—in pursuit of that eclectic magic—a legendary stage and screen performer, the third person to win the elusive EGOT (an Emmy, a Grammy, an Oscar, and a Tony) Rita Moreno with a terrific classically trained actor, who was better known for his film roles, Danny Glover.

I found them to be very different personalities. Glover struck me as very Jeff Spicoli (Sean Penn's character in *Fast Times at Ridgemont High*). He was beyond laid back. He might have been terribly shy, or introspective, or maybe just sorry he'd signed up for the gig. But it was hard to get him engaged in what we were doing that evening. Not knowing him I couldn't tell you if that was his normal way of presenting himself or not. But he was kind, he was polite, and was present. And that last one was supremely important to a live show.

Rita Moreno was just the opposite. She walked through the stage door bounding with energy and asking questions to which she expected immediate and precise answers. I hope that doesn't make it sound like she was difficult. She wasn't. When a legend lends their name to a group with which she is unfamiliar, she has an obligation to her own brand to ensure that she is presented in a professional and positive manner. If things go well, our organization looks good. If they don't, Rita Moreno is on the front page of TMZ—not me.

Glover and Moreno were each in their own orbits for most of the evening. About 15 minutes before they were to take the stage we offered them a rehearsal space in case they wanted to run through the dialogue a couple of times and maybe work up some chemistry. Nobody on my team monitored that. I mean, seriously, the director and the producers were busy. You want me to assign an intern to critique Rita Moreno's rehearsal? Not gonna happen.

As they stepped on to the stage of the Schubert Theatre there was a very hearty and well-deserved applause. All that was required of them was to read literally three lines of dialogue, and announce a winner. But then Glover calls an audible, changing the play at the last minute.

"Before we go through all this stuff, I just want to say that it is both an honor and a privilege to be standing on this stage tonight with not just a legend, but one of my personal heroes, Miss Rita Moreeeeno" Pronouncing it with a long "e" sound.

To which she answered, "Moreeeeno is a quarterback. My name is MorAYno," pronouncing it with a strong Latin flavor.

Dead, uncomfortable silence. You might be able to hear a pin drop, but the pin was way too afraid to drop. And a few seconds go by.

And there's still silence.

Danny apologizes, profusely and sincerely. I don't know exactly what happened up there. But I am 100 percent certain that he did not intend to show her anything but reverence.

Lesson

Unlike Stiller and Meara, to whom I also gave free reign, Moreno and Glover didn't know each other. There was no indication they had any personal chemistry or connection. I just thought that two great pros deserved the wide berth and would request assistance when they feel it was needed.

But Stiller and Meara were married both personally and professionally for 50 years. I should have kept an eye on these two and been available for some sort of consultation. You see, there *are* people who do not need supervision to turn out greatness— but if you don't know that's what you're dealing with—supervise.

Footnote

Most of the people in the theatre that night believed this was a pre-planned bit that they arranged during their 15 minutes in a rehearsal room. So I am in the minority when I tell you that I think it was just a moment went two talented people were on a different wavelength. I look at it logically and ask, "What would be the payoff, or the punchline?" On the other hand, are they talented enough actors to have fooled me? By a long shot. The one thing I do know is that this moment gets debated quite often amongst those of us who were there that evening. It's become our lasting backstage celebrity mystery.

Chapter Seventeen
Charlton Heston

Background

His mother was an Israelite slave who set him afloat in a basket of reeds so that he might escape the wrath of the Pharaoh's decree that... alright, the actual backstory. But that is, in a way, part of the essential Heston backstory. He was the guy who went up the mount to deliver the law unto his people. It's half of the backstory. Heston has two incredible and indelible public personas. First, he was the mythic hero of Hollywood who parted the Red Sea as Moses in *The Ten Commandments*, and road revolutionary chariots in *Ben Hur*. When I was growing up, he was just Moses. "Who's on Carson's show tonight?"

"Shecky Greene and Moses."

But by the mid-90's there was a new generation that knew him as the NRA spokesperson who famously dared us to "pry my guns from my cold dead hands." He was, in those latter days, the very symbol of the NRA and the gun lobby.

So in some sense, it seemed anathema to have him as a presenter at an L.A.-based theatre awards show. Show business is a very lefty world. And the theatre community is way to the left of even Hollywood. So when we announced him as a presenter our community shuttered. It had never occurred to me to consider someone's political stance when lining them up to give out a theatre award. Maybe I'm noble for that, perhaps stupid. Most likely both.

In the weeks leading up to the event I got calls and emails and personal visits from people who questioned my sanity. They tried to have me removed from my position. They threatened and tried to organize a boycott. And these were people who were my *friends*! I did not get a single person standing up and saying they thought this was the right decision. Not one person said, "Heston belongs on that stage" I had been told that more than half the audience was planning on getting up and walking out the moment his name was announced.

Story

Lining up Charlton Heston was no easier than dealing with the political agenda crowd. His handler—I never once spoke directly to "Chuck"—wanted to know exactly what time Heston would be presenting. Despite the fact award shows are an imprecise science, I said "10:22."

Handler answered, "Mr. Heston's car will arrive at the stage door at 10:07. He will step out of the car and into the wings at 10:17. He will proceed directly on stage, deliver his lines, and go directly back to the car. No handshakes, no backstage photos, and definitely no press."

There was no way I could agree to all that from this pain in my ass prima donna that nobody else even wanted at the stupid event. What a set of balls on him that he thinks his crap doesn't stink and that he gets his own set of rules. You know what—good for you Chuck—I hope they all walk out.

And though that's what I was thinking, I said "Absolutely. We are happy to accommodate Mr. Heston."

And sure enough, night of the show, Heston's limo pulls up to the stage door at 10:07—precisely! Ten minutes later the limo door opens, and Heston's people lift him out and set him up with a walker. *What*? He inches slowly, almost feebly, to the wings propelling himself to an inch from the audience's sightline, just in time to hear his name.

And wouldn't you freakin know it. Suddenly he's Moses. He pushes the walker aside, stands up so straight, so majestically, like a Biblical hero. He walks to the podium with a spring in his step like a teenager, and then the impossible happens. The audience stands, but instead of turning to leave, they applaud. I have been in the presence of princes, presidents, and even Prince, but I have never seen charisma like Heston in my entire life. He cocked his head and said "Hello,"— and the applause started all over again. From the people who were calling him a baby killer in the pre-show cocktail lounge!

I got a call from his handler the next day. "Mr. Heston wanted me to call and thank you for what he called one of the most revelatory evenings of his career. You see this was his first public event since his hip replacement surgery."

Lesson

The lesson here is that you never really know the whole story. I convinced myself this guy was a self-important ego driven has-been, who was screwing with me because he could. I am to this day embarrassed that I ever had those thoughts. He was a star. And I happened to catch him at a vulnerable moment where he was doing whatever he could to make *my* event work. Never assume you know the entire story. Because you most certainly do not.

Addendum

On the other hand, I once turned down the chance to be involved in a production of the play *Quilters*—about the women who created the AIDS quilt—at the Reagan Library. The event was envisioned (by Nancy Reagan I was told) as a rapprochement between President Reagan's legacy and the gay community, to address the tensions of the administration's failure to address HIV/AIDS when it first became a blight on the gay community.

The catch was that one of the performers who had done the play recently was Betty Garrett, who you might know from *On the Town*, or *All in the Family*. When I told Betty, she almost killed me. She believed that Reagan had turned her husband in to the House Un-American Activities Committee and ruined his career. (This is entirely possible, since Reagan did out people to the FBI when he was President of the Screen Actors Guild.)

I stood by Betty Garrett and let them know I was not interested in being considered.

Chapter Eighteen
Robert E. Lee and the 25 Celebrity Vaginas

Background

Most of the messages and lessons I learned in this book are timeless, because knowledge and truth really don't change all that much. But this one story, which happened over the past year, is very specific to the here and now. I don't know if today's America is more philosophically divided than we have ever been previously, but it is apparent to me that there is less willingness to think of people on the opposite side of the political spectrum as fully-realized humans, capable of complex thought. We protect our own beliefs by making the other side less human. This is an instance of that exact phenomenon, and how we saw through it.

Story

When I took my current job in May of 2017, as the CEO of The Muckenthaler Center, it was a departure for me in some ways. While the organization has a theatre and an art gallery, and produces 50 concerts, a jazz festival, a car show, and half a dozen galas in the course of a year, it also has an education department that brings the arts into prisons, homeless shelters, battered womens' facilities, and anywhere else the arts are needed and scarce. I haven't made my career in *that* world up to now.

The other big difference is that it is in Orange County, a long-time conservative stronghold. Fullerton in particular has a reputation for being a more traditional, tight-knit community with a perspective on the arts that was less than inclusive.

I was determined, when creating the 2018 performance season, to push the outer edges of the artistic boundaries. Not to lay waste to the aesthetic of the community—after all, my mission was to serve their needs and not to satisfy my personal tastes--I'm not the audience. But I wanted to see if, perhaps, inclusion was a better model for an arts center than exclusion, to make the case that the quality of the work can often trump the audience's POV.

Early on, the head of our education department proposed a one-night fundraiser for her department. She suggested a production of Eve Ensler's *Vagina Monologues*, which by special permission from Ms. Ensler, is made available during the month of February for exactly these purposes. It's an annual windfall for many 501(c) (3) organizations across America, but not so much in Fullerton, or at The Muck. Booking this event meant that the word "Vagina" was going to appear in our annual brochure. On posters. In emails sent to our members. Spoken aloud from our stage. Booking this show meant that we were going to disseminate the repeated reminder of the existence of the female genitalia in this God-fearing town over and over again.

This one scared me a little. How would our audience, which leans toward conservative senior citizens, partial to acts like The Mantovani Strings or the local high school orchestra, react to me using my first season at the helm to present so much... raw labia?

And we had peppered the show with 25 celebrity appearances from the stars of network TV shows on NBC (*Las Vegas*), Bravo (*Millionaire Matchmaker*) HGTV (*House Hunters*) and even a member of the legendary heavy metal band, Skid Row! I originally thought that would stoke ticket sales. But now I was worried that the offended would say "Damn Hollywood liberals trying to tell me how to think"

At the same, I sought to add a remarkable one-man show to our season. Tom Dugan is probably the greatest living practitioner of the art form. He's toured the world as either writer or performer in a long list of amazing shows. I'd seen his Simon Wiesenthal show (*Nazi Hunter*) where he played to a sold-out house at the 92 St Y in New York. And I was there for his wonderful Jackie Kennedy show at the Annenberg in Beverly Hills. For the Muck, I wanted to book his Robert E Lee show. In fact, I thought we'd make a giant event out of it. So, we hired Civil War re-enactors to cover our eight acres of lawn and have a daylong battle in our bluffs and around our groves. Give the neighborhood something to talk about, right?

On the one hand, I was being cautioned that, "This community will never stand for *The Vagina Monologues!* We'll lose funding and support! People here will never accept that. They're way too conservative. It just not the way we do things."

Three separate people used the same exact phrase, "You are digging your own grave"

On the other hand, there were warnings on Robert E Lee—that perhaps we shouldn't appear to be pro-confederacy or pro-slavery. There's a defiant militant liberal underbelly in town, I was told. And they would not stand for a celebration of inequality. Of course, I had seen this show and knew it was *not* those things. So, my antennae were up looking for potential trouble. And then, Charlottesville, Virginia…

Right then, thousands of miles away, in Virginia, a newly-controversial statue of General Lee was being removed, and then not removed, and then removed, from where it had stood for decades, stirring up all sorts of inflammatory rhetoric. Network news feeds were doing live remotes from the statue site. Protestors, counter protestors, counter-counter protestors. And then it got ugly. A car was driven through a crowd killing Heather Heyer, a young woman who was protesting. Suddenly General Lee was a lightning rod, and I had him on my schedule.

Not only that, but I had sold all the matinee tickets for the run to the local school districts, which seemed like a good thing when we cashed the check. Not so good when I got an email from the editor of the local newspaper.

The editor outwardly questioned my judgment (I suspect she privately questioned my sanity) in allowing a racist symbol of treason to be the focal point of an evening's entertainment. She didn't seem placated by my assurance that Lee was no more racist than Grant, and that only by learning about our adversaries can we hope to gain understanding. I begged her to first *see* the show before condemning it. I was relieved when she agreed. Not because I'd won the debate, but because her warnings in the paper would surely have made the school district squeamish and threatened to turn a big profit into a devastating financial loss.

The Vagina Monologues was advertised, promoted, performed to a sold-out house and a standing ovation. Not a single person had a negative reaction to the content.

Robert E. Lee was performed masterfully, sold out its run, and got rave reviews. And only one person complained about the content. He saw the show, admired the writing and performance, stayed for the Q and A, and still thinks I was wrong to book it.

These were the two highest grossing shows on our 2018 schedule. And the income was not fueled by controversy at all. But by excellence.

Lesson

The lesson takes some careful and subtle reading of the situation, with the exception of that last gentleman I mentioned, not a single person was offended. What did happen was many people got preemptively, vicariously, offended on the behalf of others.

Most of the noise I heard was all "they-centric." The board won't support it. The community will be upset. The audience can't accept this. With one solitary exception, not a single individual was able to say "I, myself, am offended".

At first glance the lesson might be not to assume you know how the hearts and minds of others will react. But I think there's something more important, and frankly quite timely for our society.

People have giant hearts and immense capacities. They, screw that, *we* are not the pea-brained insular bigots we all think we are. Though it is human nature to categorize and demonize the other, it is a damn good time in our history to re-examine and fight against that instinct.

I can't tell you how many political arguments I've heard in the past year where someone said, "I'd be willing to meet them halfway for a sensible compromise, but they'd never accept it". You're wrong, they would. Maybe not the fringe zealots in a movement, but the overwhelming majority would embrace reason. And they would have already except for one thing. They don't believe *you* would.

Chapter Nineteen
Lance Bass

Background

Just before I moved to New York and took over SiriusXM's OUTQ station—the first and only radio station dedicated to the LGBTQ audience—they had hired Lance Bass to do a show on that station. Lance was a pioneer among celebrities for being out while still young. And he was never afraid to campaign for causes of equality. By the same token, he's also an impossibly nice guy who made his fame and money in the notoriously not-so-nice music world as part of the band NSYNC.

I was way past the point of obsessions with pop acts when NSYNC came along, so he wasn't a guy I remembered from my youth. But I was certainly well aware of the incredible success the guys had had. Even if I didn't know the difference between them and the Backstreet Boys.

Story

Lance did his daily show from his basement in the Burbank/Glendale area. SiriusXM had built him a studio down there and paid for a producer and an engineer to work on the show with him. And when I was in L.A., part of my responsibility was to stop by and see what I could do to help that show out. What I mean by that is, doing a show from a basement, 3000 miles from the home office, leaves you feeling detached. Also, Lance didn't see himself as a gay radio host. He saw himself as a radio host covering pop music and pop culture. He never complained or rebelled, nor did he let any resentment affect his performance. But I think he simply would have preferred to have his show considered an entertainment show.

Before my first visit I was warned that Lance was a star, and needed to be treated as a star. I was told that he hired his buddy to write and help produce the show, and that contact should go through that guy. Being told all of that, my expectation was that the guy was on a 1975 Mick Jagger star trip and my only strategic maneuver was deciding which of his ass cheeks to kiss.

But that never made sense. I spoke to his team and they said, "We'll be in the basement prepping the show. We'll leave the door unlocked, just come on in." And when I pulled up, it was certainly a nice home. But it wasn't a palatial estate. Just a nice home in a residential middle class neighborhood in the suburbs. The door was unlocked, as promised. I found the basement and headed down. Again, it could have been any home in any city owned by any typical family. And there was Lance and his team, working on a show. The buddy/intermediary guy greeted me, but Lance was pretty much engaged so I didn't have a chance to say hello right away. Ah, maybe this is where the ego displays itself. Nope.

It was suggested that I look in the other room of the basement to find a chair, and when I stuck my head in there I saw something remarkable. Statues. One propping the door open. About two dozen more against the back wall. Maybe another ten leaning on the wall behind me. So I looked more closely.

They weren't statues exactly. They were awards. MTV Awards dominated, but who knows what else was down there? Golden Globes? Grammys? Billboard Awards? It was the raw material to build a Michael Phelps-ian shrine to one's self. And they were just kind of scattered around like this was a storage closet. So I asked Lance about it. He has a bit of a southern twang, and a giant sincere smile. I could tell this was a question he had answered before. He just kinda shrugged and said he didn't feel comfortable having a big room in his house where people sat around and stared at his trophies. He said it would be sad to invite people over to a room like that, and even sadder to sit in there alone. And in the very next sentence he asked if was going to still be in town on Friday, because they all hang out at the pool after the show on Fridays.

Lesson

People are who people are who people are. I don't think success goes to people's head. I tend to think that damaged people are empowered by money and fame, and healthier people seem to ride it out quite nicely.

So if you are considering training your child to be a star athlete or performer, please remain vigilant about their mental health as well. Teach them the life lessons, and decency, and empathy that you know would have served them well in a "regular" job.

Chapter Twenty
Blind Item Number One

In one of the first few years of The Ovation Awards, we had to deal with a household name level movie star who either showed up intoxicated, or over indulged at the bar before having to walk on stage. He wasn't particularly belligerent or difficult. But a little too mumbly and rambling for comfort. I sat him down and tried a direct, honest approach. I told him that it *seemed* like he may have accidently misjudged the strength of this bartender's drinks, and that it is possible neither of us would benefit from... he was already ignoring me.

He went on stage, walked to the podium, stared at the audience for an uncomfortable amount of time—probably a few seconds, but it seemed much longer—before starting with a proclamation which I will paraphrase here, "You know, I am not an alcoholic." Followed by another silence, as if he was waiting for the audience to respond.

Lesson

Sometimes you have to protect other people to protect yourself. In a different decade, such as the one we are living in today, the cell phones would have been out immediately and TMZ would have turned this into a career-threatening event for the poor guy on stage. And in turn, maybe, me.

But beyond that, maybe I shouldn't have let him go up there. It was a room full of show folk. And he came off pretty crappy. I could have helped.

Chapter Twenty-One
Blind Item Number Two

I was once producing a musical for Broadway based on the life of the legendary Notre Dame Football coach Knute Rockne. I may or may not have also written the libretto—depending on which version we were producing at the time.

Coming in to audition for the role of George Gipp (The Gipper—the role played by Ronald Reagan in the Hollywood film) was a long line of highly trained stage performers... and a graduate of a multi-platinum boy band. While he himself wasn't a household name, the band most certainly was, and we had every intention of giving him this role, even changing the role somewhat to fit him.

Our thought process was
1. We had investors and wanted to maximize their potential of a return.
2. Maybe this would bring teenage girls into the theatre?
3. Even if he was too slightly built to be believable as a star athlete, the world loved *West Side Story* and those guys didn't look like gangbangers. Theatre audiences suspend belief differently than film audiences. Those were the ways we justified

it to ourselves since the only thing we knew about him before the audition was that he could sing.

And then came the audition. And though this young man was less than inspiring, we put his headshot up on the board as one of our main candidates for a lead role. Because he was who he was, and because ticket sales, and because the press, and because investors.

And then someone spoke up. It might have been the composer, Larry O'Keefe. Or maybe the musical director, or the director. I don't remember, but someone just said, "Hold on a minute. The boy cannot fuckin' sing." We all acknowledged that, took him off the board instantly and never thought about it again.

Lesson

Speaking up, against what you think is the tide, often works. Not because you suddenly turn the hearts and minds of a crowd with stunning oratory. It usually works because everyone was thinking the same thing and didn't pipe up.

Chapter Twenty-Two
Blind Item Number Three

I was taking two of my most successful radio hosts on a publicity tour to New York City. These two ladies had worked together for almost a decade and like most hosting teams, loved each other... And hated each other. Both rather intensely.

They were much more partiers on these trips than I was. My own particular peculiarities made me want to not endanger the respect I had earned as their boss, by going out all night and acting like an idiot. Which is what I do when I allow myself to go out all night... which is why I don't ... OK, we're caught in a bit of a loop here.

Three o'clock a.m. my cell phone rings. I guess one of the girls had a new boyfriend who had flown in from L.A. to see her. He took both girls to a club way downtown. I can't vouch for any of the details because the person telling them to me was intoxicated enough to misconstrue them, and crying hard enough to distort them, and I was half asleep. But here's what I got:

All three were drinking... the guy took a body shot off a waitress... his girlfriend/my host got jealous... Big argument, the guy left... the two girls are sobbing on a street corner. They want me to get in a taxi and come get them.

It's Manhattan! Cabs are everywhere; they don't need me. But as anyone who has ever had to deal with talent will tell you, there are times when you just have to stop holding on to logic.

I put on pants, grabbed a cab in midtown, and found the girls screaming at each other in SoHo. "Get in the cab."

"But she—"

"Get in the cab."

"Let me tell you what the—"

"Get in the cab"

"I don't have enough money to pay for—"

"*Get. In. The. Cab.*"

We head back to the hotel in silence for about 15-20 blocks until the girlfriend turns to the other woman and says, "Nobody is ever going to love me, and it's your fault"

"Me?" Says the other girl.

"Yeah, because you're a whore. And they think because I hang around with you that I'm a whore"

I could sense that this situation was not going to right itself within the next few minutes. I was in the front seat with the cabbie. The two girls were in the back, fighting. Physically fighting. One of them had opened the cab door and was trying to push the other out as we speed through New York's streets in the wee hours. There's grunting, and shrieking, and screaming.

The cabbie asked me, "What do you want me to do?"

I said. "Uh… roll tape"

Lesson

I was right to distance myself. Not because this night ultimately descended into insanity. Most evenings didn't. But because you need to keep a professional distance from employees. Even well balanced ones.

Chapter Twenty-Three
Stormy Daniels and Karen MacDougal

Background

As the guy in charge of radio stations that had porn stars, strippers, nude models and playmates, as fulltime hosts, not just as guests, I got to know quite a few of the young ladies fairly well—in the business sense—wait, that doesn't sound good. This included thousands of on-air hours, and thousand more off-air, where the young ladies would talk about all kinds of things. But most of those things related to sex.

Off air, I have had women tell me about their affairs with ball players, actors, rock stars, rappers and politicians. I might be able to throw 100 names out there that you would recognize. In fact, several of the girls told me about meeting Donald Trump.

But none of those women were Stormy Daniels.

Story

Stormy was a hard booking to get in those days. She was what was called "a contract girl." She had an exclusive agreement with an adult film company and they restricted her appearances to those that were beneficial to the company. Understandable. But she was a big name and we wanted to book her. So, what we did was go through her husband (at the time). Mike was, and is, a straight up guy and one of the few professional publicists working with adult entertainers that could be trusted.

Whenever Stormy came in from Florida, where they lived, she dropped by the studio for a while. She was always dressed in a business suit—and ok, sometimes the skirts were a little short, or there was an extra button open on the blouse.

She was happy to talk about any subject that came up. And she remained open and charming. What she wouldn't do, where she wouldn't go, was where so many of the others from her line of work did. She wasn't interested in participating in demonstrations or lewd games, to the point where you might actually think she was a bit of a prude.

Not at all. She had a mindset that physical contact of a sexual nature was quite literally her business. And if that were to happen, there would need to be a negotiation about how she would be compensated *and* before that could happen she would need to clear it through the company with whom she had an exclusive deal.

I don't know anything about her affair with President Trump, including whether or not it happened, only that I have no doubt her approach to the entire endeavor was entirely professional. If she sought to renegotiate those terms later, when it was more advantageous for her to do so, that would be in character, and in fact, it would not be unlike Mr. Trump's countless renegotiations with creditors over the years.

Karen MacDougal was a completely different personality. I knew her even less well than I knew Stormy. But she came through the studio a few times to be on air with us.

She was as stunning a woman as you could ever meet. And pleasant, and real and engaging. I remember once being in a room where Karen was among several Playmates who were single, and talking about an agreement to fix each other up with someone. This wasn't anything out of the ordinary, other than how humanizing it was to see these icons of beauty not feeling they had the options at their fingertips to find a desirable mate.

I imagine that when her Trump story became public she was hurt. I suspect she was hurt by the invasion of her privacy, about the knowledge that her Trump-time coincided with others, that he would deny it, and that it didn't mean to him what it meant to her.

Lesson

The lesson here is that when given the same stimuli, we each react differently. It's based on who we are and where we have been. Stormy and Karen are somewhat intertwined in these scandal stories, but what led up to them, how their alleged affairs were conducted, and the reaction to it becoming public are polar opposites.

Chapter Twenty-Four
Blind Item Number Four

Don't you love stories that start with, "I was at the airport with my producer and my publicist, waiting for a flight to Reno to inspect a brothel?"

Well I was. It was the Southwest Terminal at Burbank and we had to wait for the passengers to disembark from the incoming flight from Vegas, before we could fly out to Reno—where the brothel was.

If you've ever taken Southwest, you know they operate a lot like a New York City subway in that as people try to get off the plane, the next group of passengers crowds around hoping to be the first ones on. Because Southwest, like the NYC subway, has no assigned seats. It shouldn't matter on the plane. Nobody will have to stand. But they've created this psychological impediment to orderly business.

Anyway, coming off the plane from Vegas was a familiar face. At that time, she might have been the single most famous reality star on television. Not just naturally beautiful, but well made-up at this particular moment.

The publicist who was with me had been her publicist. The producer who was with me had been her producer. And I had been in dozens of face-to-face

93

conversations with her. She wasn't someone we kinda sorta knew. This was someone we had all had a friendly relationship with.

As she comes off the plane, our eyes meet hers. Our three faces light up, thrilled to see her. She looks right through us.

The publicist says her name, and she keeps walking.

The producer says, "Hey, it's us." And says *our* names. She keeps walking.

So I said, "Not even a hello for old friends?."

She stopped, turned back, with a disgusted expression and gave a derisive half-snort in our direction.

Lesson

She has gotten into a few public rows with her former castmates. Each has written a tell-all book which included demonizing the others. If that's what you need to sell your book, to feed your family, or even to exorcise your demons, fine. But since that incident I have offered every single one of her castmates a solid paying gig on the radio. Except her. Not because I hold a grudge, but because I simply can't risk allowing that level of unprofessional behavior through my door.

If she called today I would be thrilled to meet her for lunch. Or have her over the house one day. But I won't hire her.

Chapter Twenty-Five
Blind Item Number Five

I was at the engagement party of two of the brightest young stars on the Broadway scene. They are both brilliant, and they are both delightful. I was honored to attend both their engagement party and their wedding.

The engagement party was held at one of the swankiest hotels in this city. Yes. I could have said "elegant," or "prestigious," but swankiest really hits the mark. Thick oak panels and lots of marble. Waiters in tuxedoes. Every man in a tie… except me.

There was a surprise element to the evening. A couple of them actually. The groom was surprising the bride with the party, she thought it was going to be a nice quiet dinner for two. So we were hiding, a couple dozen of us, in the restrooms. For more than an hour.

I made friends with a gentleman—not something I often do in restrooms—who had known the happy couple even longer than I had. He asked what I do and I explained that while I write and produce Broadway shows, I had this other career that I don't talk about often in such polite society settings. He said, "We're in the restroom."

I explained my Playboy gig, and that while I was

far from ashamed of it, mentioning it always leads to people talking about their weird sex habits. I didn't want that to happen at a pal's engagement party.

The guy I was talking to understood. In fact, he said. "I get it. But you don't have to worry about me. My girlfriend and I are swingers. We have been to our fair share of sex parties."

Right, like I said, it makes people start talking about that stuff. Anyway, we talked a bit more. Turned out we knew a few of same perverts. And the end of the evening we exchanged business cards.

Lesson

There doesn't seem to be much of a lesson, does there? That's because I didn't give you the postscript to the story. Today, that guy, who spent an hour in the bathroom telling me about him and his swinger girlfriend is a household-name politician. I see him fairly regularly on the Sunday morning news shows.

Now you probably think the lesson is "don't tell people your secrets, it'll come back to haunt you." But that isn't a lesson I learned in this story. And besides, it has not come back to haunt him at all. The guy has a squeaky clean reputation as far as I can tell.

The lesson is that I never took him seriously. I watched him climb up the political ladder, one rung at a time, always sure some less honorable bastard than me would come splashing this dirt in the papers. I think the lesson learned here is that while we all have our foibles, what the public despises most, is the hypocrite. A fire and brimstone preacher who runs sex parties loses face. A guy who campaigns against gay rights and get arrested soliciting men in an airport bathroom loses a career. But this particular guy—either by defensive design or by his natural inclination—doesn't base his career on restoring the sanctity to marriages in America. So he's immune. That's the lesson. Sincerity covers sins.

Chapter Twenty-Six
Johnny Dawkins and/or Michael Jordan

Background

I am a big sports fan. I follow hockey in an insane level of detail. And baseball as well. I've played them both for years in rec leagues and coached kids in both sports. I started playing soccer when my daughter did so I could understand the game. I tried tennis, a little bit of Brazilian Jiu Jitsu. And as a spectator I love football, boxing, just about anything in the Olympics. I even once attended a World Championship Chess match. It almost doesn't matter what the sport is, I am interested.

The exception is basketball. I could go in to a long explanation of why it isn't an actual sport, but my fantasy is that one day I get the chance to make that into its own book. Maybe I can stop it from being played across the globe. That's unlikely—but if I can just save one child from the horrors of basketball, it would be a life well lived.

This story is impossible to comprehend unless you grasp that a person who can give you the starting rotation of a couple minor league baseball teams, hasn't watched a professional basketball game since

Rick Barry was playing for the New York Nets in a league that has not existed for decades.

Story

We'll get back to basketball in a minute. But the story starts when I skipped out on college graduation in Buffalo, New York to go on a blind date weekend in Chapel Hill, North Carolina. It mattered little to me in the moment that my mother had worked incredibly hard to get me through school. We could not afford it, and I wasn't particularly good at it.

She deserved to see me graduate. And that might have possibly happened, if my best friend wasn't dating a girl who had a friend... in North Carolina. Whatever apologies I owe her for yet another escapade, get lost in the torrent of selfish decisions.

North Carolina is *so* hot at the beginning of June it is impossible to experience the locale as a human. Within a day I looked like a sweaty lobster, and felt like a ragged burning hot plate. So it wasn't really my thing when someone signed us up to participate in a charity tennis tournament. It must have been the parents of one of the girls. It feels like it might have been something a dad wanted to do... until the weather. And then he dumped it on me.

But I'm a guest, and obligated to choose either tennis of golf. Tennis seemed shorter in duration and closer to medical help. So tennis it was.

My buddy and I were paired up with two celebrities. Me and one celeb, against my buddy and the other one. We got introduced, we were told they were basketball players, and my mind went blank.

Who cares? I only remember that their names sounded similar in cadence. So when you spoke them aloud they sounded almost the same.

Just before we started, some big shot came over to me and said something like "You scored dude, you get to play with Johnny Dawkins."

Ok, so now I've got two guys, one on my team, one on the other. And only one name between them. Johnny Dawkins.

So we played for two hours and I called both guys by the full name, the whole time. They were both "Johnny Dawkins"

"Nice shot, Johnny Dawkins."

"Your serve, Johnny Dawkins."

"And Johnny Dawkins hits a winner past Johnny Dawkins and we're back at deuce."

I can't imagine what Johnny Dawkins and Johnny Dawkins must have thought of me. Did they think I was making a weird racist statement about black guys all looking a like? They could have been Richard Petty and Richard Petty for all I cared. I didn't get how two guys I never heard of were celebrities or why I was forced to play tennis with them. It didn't seem very charitable.

Dawkins and I beat my friend and his Dawkins.

After the match one of the girls came over to tell us how cool it was that we just played tennis with the kid who just started in the NBA, who was a great college player blah blah blah. They lived down there so they cared about basketball, and worse, college basketball.

I have to tell you, I do not know to this day if they were correct in telling me that the other guy was

Michael Jordan. Both Johnny Dawkins' were a foot taller than us and 73 times better than us as athletes. But my story is that I played, and defeated, the supposed greatest athlete in the world, Michael Jordan.

Lesson

There was another day more than a decade later, when I just happened to be playing golf—which I don't do often. But this was a chance to play a simple par three with some drunk priests. Cannot pass that up. That same day there was a story in the press about Jordan losing a few hundred grand on a round of golf when he shot a 94. That day I shot a 92. OK, I get that par on my course was 54 and it was 72 for him. That's not the point. The point was that in the time where people were calling Michael Jordan the greatest athlete in the world I defeated him in both golf and tennis. Two very different sports, requiring vastly different skill sets. And furthermore, I know of no other day where Jordan shot a better round of golf than I did, nor did he ever avenge the tennis loss.

I can lay claim to dethroning Jordan as the World's Greatest Athlete.

And yes. I am well aware that this whole story is preposterous.

But that is the lesson. That it is perfectly fair game to indulge one's soul in the preposterous. To be able to sew together disparate facts and weave a blanket of athletic invincibility is a worthwhile lark.

You have to be truthful in court. You have to be truthful in relationships. You have to be truthful on your resume and when writing books. So, once in a while, take the leap and lie to yourself.

101

Addendum

I've also gotten the chance to share an ice rink with NHL players, and tried to return the serve a of professional tennis player. Once I'm done lying to myself, I make sure to remind myself how many massive steps ahead of me even the worst professional athlete is.

Chapter Twenty-Seven
Chippendales

Background

My wife and I got married on a yacht, on the five-year anniversary of our first date, and honeymooned in Paris. Which sounds very lovely. And it really was very lovely. I have almost-fluency in conversational Spanish. Touristy stuff. Enough to direct a cab driver or order in a restaurant. But neither of us spoke a word of French. In fact, for a year before the wedding I drove around L.A. with a cassette tape in the car that was supposed to be teaching me rudimentary French. Yes, a cassette tape. Which did not teach me much French, but it does prove I'm probably older than you are.

Story

We're about a week into the trip. We had explored most of the key "must-see" sights of the French capital from our love nest on Rue du Temple in the Marais. After exploring Sacre-Coeur, we found a local restaurant—seemingly the most authentic, non-tourist trap, filled-with-locals place we could have stumbled upon in all of Paris. There was a wait for a table and so we slipped into a pub across the street for a drink while we waited.

It was a long thin storefront, and we were seated near the entrance. But I could hear, from way in the back, something I had not heard in what seemed like forever. Could it be? Am I hallucinating from hunger and homesickness? *No*! There's actually people speaking English somewhere in this place!

Now it wasn't *real* English, the kind we speak in America. It was a cheap British knockoff version. But the idea that we could communicate with someone other than each other felt welcoming. So we introduced ourselves to what looked like a bunch of hard-drinking cockney soccer hooligans. They had had a couple before we arrived and planned on a few more. But they were welcoming us with open arms.

I explained that this was our honeymoon and asked what they were doing.

"We're doin' a show"

"What show?"

"We was just in Berlin, and then Amsterdam, and now 'ere"

That doesn't tell me what show so I asked again. "What's the name of it?"

"You ain't seen it. Quite sure"

"I produce theatre for a living. If you're touring Europe in a show, it's pretty likely I know it."

"We ain't in it. I run da lights. Billy runs sounds. We is the crew"

"What kind of show?"

"You might like it. It's got awl kinds a dancing and music and whatnot. Lotsa lightin' effects"

"Music and... but what?"

"Tells ya what. Openin' night is tomorrow. 'Appy to leaves you a couple tickets at the door, if you'd like?"

"Sure. Opening night of a show in Paris."

We accepted the offer and went back across the street to dinner and had a meal I hated because I had ordered the wrong thing due to misunderstanding the menu. Which was in French.

But maybe the language barrier was just as great in English, because although I knew the time and place of the show we would be seeing the next night, I still didn't know what show it was.

So the next evening we got all dressed up in the best clothes we had with us, and got into a taxi that took us across arrondissement after arrondissement until we were back near where we had the met the boys last night.

There's a line outside. Those giant searchlights that send beams up into the night sky. There's a giant marquee. This is the place. But as I look up and actually *read* the marquee, it all becomes quite clear.

This is a Chippendale's show. The crew guys were at the door laughing at me and, sure, why not. I just brought my wife to a male strip show on our honeymoon.

Lesson

When something smells weird, keep asking questions. I was happy to get tickets to a show, and didn't want to insult the new friends. But I really should have asked more questions before I agreed to go on this kind of adventure.

Addendum

The oddest thing about being an American and seeing male strip shows in Europe is (granted that is after you accept the fact that you're seeing a male strip show on your honeymoon) the cultural divide. For instance, the costumes and scenarios are the same clichéd silliness you would expect. But the Euro guys looked so awkward trying to be something so stereotypically American that you had to laugh. There was a cowboy who climbed on his wooden horse the way a four year-old mounts a merry go-round horse.

Here are some stories I borrowed from my family. From my two grandfathers, and then one from my mother, to be exact. Because they aren't *my* stories, I leave off personal addenda.

Chapter Twenty-Eight
Donald Trump

Background

My father's father, Al Hirsch, was a builder in New York City in the middle decades of the 20th Century. Not on any grand scale. His general M.O. was to buy a small plot of land in Brooklyn or Queens as they were growing. These lots could house a couple of homes, maybe a small six-unit apartment building.

I would guess that he might have been one of hundred guys doing the exact same thing on the exact same scale. But a hundred guys doing the same thing, in the same fairly confined geographic area, is a very small world and everyone knew everyone. Either personally, or at least by reputation.

Story

And this is how my grandfather knew Donald Trump's father. I remember my grandfather telling me stories about this guy. Not very nice stories. He told me that Fred Trump was as bigoted a man as he had ever met and that Fred Trump was in the Klan, since somewhat substantiated by *Vice*'s Mike Pearl in the appropriately titled "All the Evidence we could find about Fred Trump's Involvement with the KKK."

He told me Trump was a Nazi who made believe he was Swedish in order to persecute Jewish tenants. Trump was indeed born in Germany, and acknowledged that his Swedish claim was false in a 1999 *New York Times* article by Tracie Rozhon; Fred and Donald settled a housing discrimination suit with the Department of Justice in 1973, promising not to discriminate against potential renters on the basis of their being black.

What my grandfather disliked most about Fredrick Christ Trump was not the potential complex he could have gotten from his middle name, or his macro worldviews on race. The latter (at least) was probably not unusual for a man born in Germany in 1905.

It was the way he treated individuals. There was a particular brand of meanness that he told me about that rolled off my back at the time. But I guess Fred had a habit of mocking and belittling people to their face. He supposedly would let go a constant torrent of personal insults, and would physically imitate a person in a way that belittled their background, their appearance, their ethnicity.

I haven't thought about these conversations with my grandfather in decades. Why would I? I never met any of the Trumps, and the only one in the story is deceased. And truth be told, my grandfather wasn't an unimpeachable source.

But I started thinking about them again during the Republican primary campaign of 2016. And of course you're a step or two ahead of what you're reading. But when Donald Trump criticized Megyn Kelly for "having blood coming out of her wherever." And when Donald Trump, during a press conference, contorted his body to make fun of a physically handicapped reporter who asked him a question. And when Donald Trump called a primary opponent "Little Marco." Or when Donald Trump talked about deporting all Muslims and punishing women who had abortions, and how most Latino immigrants were criminals. All of that had a familiar ring to it.

Lesson

Cliché-ridden lessons abound. Pick one. The most obvious is "The apple doesn't fall far from the tree" or as we say in my home, "The snot doesn't fall far from the nose." And while I do not have any firsthand knowledge of anything Fred Trump may have done, his son must have learned his boorish behavior from someone.

We have all watched endless months of his uncivil behavior during the Presidential campaign of 2016. Some people think that will make him a great President. Others think it makes hit unfit to serve in the position. So maybe the best cliché is "beauty is in the eye of the beholder."

Or maybe it is something more Biblical. Maybe it is something about judging a son for the sins of the father.

Chapter Twenty-Nine
Truman Capote

Background

My mother's father was Nathan Winograd and we were pretty close. After a couple of heart attacks my grandparents moved from Brighton Beach, Brooklyn to West Hollywood, California.

They probably came to visit us in New York about once a year or so, but this was around the time of my parent's divorce and we didn't have enough money to fly the family out to see them nearly that often.

Story

We did go to California as a family once, somewhere in the mid to late 70's. We stayed at my grandparent's apartment in West Hollywood and had breakfasts at the old Farmer's Market (Pre-Grove, if you know L.A.).

Strolling through like goofy tourists, I noticed my grandfather staring into a candy store widow. My mother asked what had gotten his interest, and he said "That's Truman Capote."

My grandfather wasn't an avid reader of literature, nor particularly hip to the social scene. I'm sure he knew Capote best as a frequent Merv Griffin guest. Retired men of that era might well have been watching Merv, or Dinah, or something like that. But I'm surprised a guy with no interest in *any* celebrities suddenly was transfixed by a guy who, how shall we say this, has certain personal affectations that working men of my grandfather's generation did not fully respect.

Nonetheless my grandfather walked directly into the candy shop, tapped him on the shoulder and said, kinda like Studs Terkel might have, "Hey, Capote!" Both friendly, and aggressive.

Capote spun around sheepishly. Looked my Grandfather in the eye and said, "Hey, how have you been?"

What do you know? Truman Capote thinks he recognizes my grandfather and starts asking personal questions. "How have you been? Is Myra with you? Is she still upset with Georgia? I bet she is. People were saying you were out here now, but nobody knows where.

It didn't last much longer than that. My grandfather didn't have much of plan beyond, "Hey, Capote." So after he stared at the writer for a little while, Capote walked away with a dismissive shrug, saying, "I might have thought you were someone else."

Lesson

I hear people say this all the time, but I find this to be a good example of the "fake it 'til you make it" school of thought. Without lying, or deceiving, or misleading, my grandfather had struck up a conversation with an American literary icon.

Had he had any inclination to do so, he might well have struck up a friendship. Just by walking up and saying hello.

Chapter Thirty
Neil Sedaka

Background

My mother grew up on Coney Island Avenue in Brighton Beach in Brooklyn. The neighborhood is famous for the number of talented people who grew up within a few blocks of each other. Barbara Streisand, Neil Diamond, Carol King. The roster is long. And it also includes another guy who was a huge star, that doesn't get remembered as much today, Neil Sedaka.

Story

My mother grew up in the world of stoopball and D.A. (duck's ass) haircuts. And though I obviously wasn't there, I imagine it resembled a non-musical version of the movie, *Grease,* except with much dirtier sidewalks and no guarantee of a happy ending. Or maybe it was more like *West Side Story*, but the gang guys were less talented in ballet.

The apartment building she grew up in had a thin slice of concrete they called the backyard. I don't want to make it sound like a squalor-filled tenement. It was also about 50 yards from one of the world's most famous beaches.

In the next building over, there lived a young man named Neil Sedaka. And every late afternoon and early evening—weather permitting—the neighborhood kids would gather on the street out front or in the backyard and play some semblance of a sport.

The way my mother tells the story, every evening, without fail, there was thick New York Jewish accent wafting through the courtyard, "Neeeee—Yillll" *Neeeeee-yillllllll."*

His mommy was calling him.

"It's time to study yer piana," or, translated into English, "It is time to study your piano."

And he was ridiculed, and derided, and rejected, and embarrassed, and put down and…

And every day when his mother called him he went anyway.

Some kids might have fought it.

I would have fought it.

My ten year-old would fight it.

But every day little Neil Sedaka picked himself up and went back inside to study his piyana.

His mother wanted him to be a classical composer like her hero, Van Cliburn. Not a pop star like Neil's cousin, Eydie Gormé. My grandparents, Nat and Hilda, were friendly with the Sedakas, Mac and Eleanor, from the neighborhood and from synagogue. So I have a little inside info on these kinds of things.

The perception at the time among the other kids (at least) was that Eleanor was demanding and overbearing. That she was forcing her son to study an instrument he had already learned, at the expense of a social life, at the expense of a "normal" childhood.

The perception of Neil was that he was... henpecked. I get the feeling that other kids rooted for him to one day get up the nerve to stand up to his mother and demand the right to be a child.

And he might still be remembered that way by the kids on Coney Island Avenue except for one amazing thing. By the time he was about 14 he was putting out hit records. OK, just sort of reginal hits at first—but what were *you* doing at 14?

He teamed up with another kid on the block, Howie Greenfield to write pop songs... like his cousin, Eydie Gormé. And by time he graduated high school Neil and his band, The Cookies, were making a living at music.

Lesson

If you're a parent, don't lose sight of the price of greatness.

Is it worth sacrificing a large portion of one's childhood? Asked that way, no.

But is it worth losing a few hours a week on an elementary school playground to have an artistically fruitful career and a few dozen million in the bank?

There may not be a right answer. But it most certainly *is* right to ask yourself those questions.

Chapter Thirty-One
Alan Zweibel

Background

I moved to Los Angeles on August 20th 1987 to become a TV writer. I would have been OK writing films, but I preferred TV. For my group of friends, there probably wasn't a more revelatory comedic influence than *Saturday Night Live*. We had all enjoyed comedy and admired funny people before. But *SNL*, in its original form, was so seemingly new that we gravitated to it.

It seems so... doable.

It seemed so... of our culture.

I Love Lucy, and *The Honeymooners* were someone else's comedy. They didn't belong to us. As much as we did respect them. *Happy Days*, well... you weren't going to re-enact a *Happy Days* scene at school the next day like you did with an *SNL* skit.

"Cheeburger Cheeburger Cheeburger Cheeburger Cheeburger Cheeburger," was our war cry.

Alan Zweibel was one of the writers of the original series.

Story

Around September 1st of 1987, I was living in L.A. for all of a few weeks, with no real plans other than to become a writer, with Eric. Maybe without, but the plan was with. I was living with my Uncle Fred, who was… less forgiving of the artistic temperament than my mother had been. He was one of this kids giving Neil Sedaka crap on the street corner in the last story. And he hadn't softened up much since.

On the other hand, I was certainly in need of some guidance, and sitting around waiting for someone I didn't know to hire me was not going be productive.

Fred called an old friend of his, who was married to a lawyer at William Morris. Who set us up with a meeting with an agent. Who said to me, "I want you to call my client, Alan Zweibel. He went to the same college as you. He will be your mentor. I told him you'll call tomorrow."

Today I would say, that agent, Mike Peretzia, gave me a golden freaking ticket.

But if you read the part of this book where I told you I was an idiot, this is a prime example.

My first thought was "Yuck, the last thing I need is a mentor. I don't want a mentor, I want a job. Writing is an art form and nobody should tell you how to do it." My second thought was, "I thought this guy was an agent. Agents are supposed to find people work, not set them up with a guru. This guy is blowing me off!"

Never stopped to consider that I didn't earn or deserve a job.

Really. That was me.

My third thought was, "And now I really have to call this guy, this Zweibel guy, who I'm sure is dreading the whole thing and has to be nice to me to appease his agent. "

So I didn't call the next as I was told. I waited about a week.

I'm an idiot.

But when I did call Alan Zweibel he was graceful and helpful and… maybe nurturing was the best word to describe it. He said he was going out of town for a few days but asked me to call him in about ten days, mid-September, 1987, and he would buy me lunch and "welcome me to L.A., officially"

And I said I would.

Did I mention my idiocy?

My next contact with Alan Zweibel was about 2008.

I was running a radio station and received a press release from a publishing house about a new title, *The Other Schulman*. It was a comedic novel about a middle-aged man who decides to train for a marathon. And it was written by… Alan Zweibel.

When Zweibel came in he was every bit as delightful in person as he had been on the phone. He talked about Gilda, told stories about Billy Crystal, and, of course, plugged the book. He stayed on the air with us for an hour. And that's unheard of in radio.

During a break in the show I introduced myself and told him the story from 1987, with Uncle Fred, and Mike Peretzia, and everything. You know what he said?

"Stop beating yourself up. You're not an idiot. You're a schmuck. It's different."

Lesson

There are only so many golden opportunities presented to you. They come mostly when you are young. People want to help the energetic and wide-eyed kids. They wanted to be able to say they gave you a step up. Once you have "made it," everybody offers help with an expectation of a quid pro quo. Which is actually quite fair.

And when you're later in your career, frankly, you're a bad investment. Helping you later on means either they are helping "a loser," or someone who won't stick it out long enough to return the favor.

I'm not advocating for anything Machiavellian. I'm not suggesting you over-exploit every resource, and leave the ground barren in your wake. But do not treat casually the truly golden chances, for they may not come again.

Chapter Thirty-Two
Sir Ian McKellen

Background

Sir Ian McKellen is the kind of actor America just doesn't produce. And you might say, "Theater-first actors? What about Mandy Patinkin, what about Nathan Lane, what about Bernadette Peters, what about Brain Stokes Mitchell? Fine point, but that group is really musical theater-first.

Can you think of an American dramatic actor who is a theatre-first performer? You might say Tim Robbins? Phillip Seymour Hoffman? Well OK, but they never sound right doing iambic pentameter and they just don't have that thing, that fun, theatre-as-adventure thing.

You know what most American actors don't have? Britishness. That natural state of carrying one's self with the utmost seriousness, while being abjectly absurd.

A wonderful example of that is Sir Ian. In consecutive years he came through town in very different productions. First, his one man show, *A Knight Out in L.A.*. It was a brave and brilliant examination of his career in which he is comedic and candid on stage about his sexuality in a way that is perfectly matter of fact. That is the standard of the 21st Century. But that wasn't so when he toured the show.

The next year he starred in a touring British production of Ibsen's *The Enemy of the People*. Ibsen can be as dour to the American ear as a Nordic winter evening. But it is brilliant political commentary about how state-led persecution of the individual can kill a man and infect a nation.

Story

The opening night party for *Enemy of the People* was on the plaza outside the Ahmanson Theatre in L.A. My wife had a table of some theatrical renown… and some flowing libations. We were sitting with the managers of Sir Ian's one-man show, Mrs. Shropshire and Mr. Wolverine (and their respective spouses). Our table also included the gentleman who ran another prestigious theatre and his beautiful wife—a performer in her own right. And the publicist for the Ibsen show we had just seen.

For no apparent reason our liquid-aided conversation became a heated discussion about the merits of male circumcision. One woman considered it a mutilation of the male organ. Someone touted the hygienic benefits, but was rebutted by others who called it hogwash. It got defended on the grounds of tradition and freedom, and derided on the grounds of being akin to voodoo.

Now this was all happening, loudly, on a plaza filled with a couple hundred people in formal wear who all knew each other from being at *every* theatre opening in L.A. So each of us arguing was undoubtedly embarrassing ourselves in front of a collection of friends and peers. Lovely.

It is something I do regularly, as you can tell from this book. My friends are usually better than that. But not on this night.

Mrs. Shropshire spotted Sir Ian walking across the plaza near us. As I said, she had worked closely with him the previous year, and knew him well. She called him over.

"Sir Ian McKellen will break the tie, won't you Sir Ian?"

"It's a bow tie, I'm not sure I can…"

"Sir Ian, we were discussing circumcision. We need you to weigh in. Are you for or against?

And this is the spot where being British is so valuable. What he said might have worked from John Gielgud, or Patrick Stewart. But not really from Tom Hanks or Denzel Washington.

He said it slowly, pausing between each word. Deadpan.

"My dear… circumcision…"

And we hung on every syllable.

"Circumcision… is…"

And people from other tables who were either amused or appalled at our banter for the past hour, were now either amused or appalled that Sir Ian was weighing in.

"Circumcision… is… the enemy of the peepee."

And there you go. Brilliant, decisive, funny, and keeping in the theme of the evening.

Don't you just want to invite *that* guy to every party you ever have?

Lesson

The lesson here is the power of wit. While clearly there are times when it is best to shut up, or to be serious, there are also times when having the ability to wrap up a thought with a tight little bow is priceless.

Oh, and the delivery of that wit. Some have the power to transcend the utterances of insults and off-color remarks. Know on which side of the fence you reside. Don't guess, *know*.

If you are the type that genuinely gets away with an occasional bawdy remark, or a clever dig at a friend, then keep that as a valued weapon in your arsenal. But unless you are sure that your rakish smile will allow you to walk out scot-free, just try not being a douchebag.

Chapter Thirty-Three
Steve Martin vs. Kelsey Grammar

Background

Not a WWE cage match. Not even a celebrity tennis match. But in successive years I had the opportunity to oversee the production of a video that would open The Ovation Awards. I've already told you about the year that George Takei did the voice over for the project. In the succeeding two years it was done by Kelsey Grammar and Steve Martin.

In all fairness, this is really my wife's story, not mine. She is the producer we hired to create the video and the one who had the most hands-on experience with the two gentlemen.

But as California is a community property state, I have the right to exploit half of the story. So here it goes.

Story

Any time a name celebrity agrees to do something like this, lend their talent to a charitable cause, it is the result of someone calling in a favor. The celebrities perform gratis due to some combination of repaying a favor, friendship, guilt and once in a blue moon… belief in the cause.

Beloved L.A. producer Joan Stein was able to secure us Steve Martin and this was a game changer kind of name for us. He was coming off a legitimate theatre success with *Picasso at The Lapin Agile*, but of course he was also not just a household name but a… what is more intensely famous and respected than a household name? Got it. He is more than a household name. He is a star in every room and hallway of the household including the attic, basement and crawlspace.

Anyway, Martin helped arrange a recording studio where my wife met him for a recording session. The script isn't very long. It is basically, "My name is Steve Martin and I would like to welcome you to the 19 whatever Theater L.A. Ovation Awards. The only peer-judged awards given by our community. Tonight's nominees were selected from over 1500 shows, by our panel of 72 judges. And here are our nominees…"

That's the whole thing.

Martin read the script over as they went to the studio. As he clearly had before. He was just being extra thorough. And then he asked several million questions in the pursuit of both excellence, and pleasing the director… who was my very talented wife, but who a lesser man might have dismissed.

"How do you want me to say this word?"

"Where should I punch this sentence?"

"So what's on the screen when I'm saying this part?"

"This opens the show, right? Cold open? And what follows it?"

"You don't want funny Steve Martin, right? Because I'm not getting any jokes from this copy."

"So just straight, right, like I'm an announcer?"

"Do you want a Gary Owens announcer, or just as though it's a documentary?"

"Is it OK if my dog stays in the studio? We do everything together?"

"Should we share an iced tea and talk about it?"

I'm not sure how many of those questions my wife anticipated before he asked, but the session went well, so her answers must have worked. Because frankly, I would have just let Steve Martin do whatever he pleased on the basis of him being Steve Martin. But my wife has more of that kind of integrity and ran through exactly what she envisioned.

Martin did about a dozen takes, with a variety of choices. And even offered to do more if these didn't work out.

The following year, through Lars Hanson and the Pasadena Playhouse, we had the opportunity to have Kelsey Grammar voice the opening video. Kelsey has a long successful theater career both before and after *Frasier*. And had recently starred in Sondheim's *Sweeny Todd*. Plus, that voice. His voice is commanding and distinct. A great choice for the "job."

Grammar was just as charitable in agreeing to perform the task. Equally giving of his time. But there was a difference.

At that point in history, Kelsey's time was not his own. Whereas Steve Martin's schedule allowed him to commit a block of time, and mental energy to the project. Kelsey was starring on a network TV show.

And he agreed to do it and I jumped. Even though

we were warned that he would fit it in when he could. And we were warned that there would be only one session, and that was TBD. And we were warned that it wasn't realistic to be able to have one of our people in the room during recording to either coach, or direct or answer questions. And though we could send written notes, there was no promise that they would be read. Time is too precious.

What we got back was three takes. With that deep booming voice, and that professional air about it.

It was good. But it wasn't exactly what we needed. Not optimally, anyway.

Now here are the realities of gathering celebrities for a charitable event.

One of our board members called in a big favor. So we are going to use this tape, and cannot ask for revisions.

A big star went out of his way to help. So we are going to use this tape, and not ask for revisions.

I was the one who made the call that we would trade some control, for the value of the name performer. So we are going to use that tape.

We were past the point where the decision could have been reversed without political headache. And, Grammar actually did a fine job. It just wasn't as good as the one Steve Martin had done the previous year.

And again, in his defense, it wasn't about talent. It was about opportunity.

Lesson

Life is a sum of the choices you make. And for a program like The Ovation Awards there was great ongoing value to having had both these gentlemen donate their time to the cause. But the evening was designed as a salute to the excellence of our community.

With that in mind, I should have erred on the side of excellence, rather than the side of notoriety. I should have had the confidence to believe that the star of the evening was the show we were producing, and the ones we were honoring.

Chapter Thirty-Four
David Hyde Pierce

Background

I hope this comes out as a compliment, it is meant as one. But when I watched David Hyde Pierce on television, I always found him hilarious, but out of place. He just felt so much more like a theatre guy to me.

I didn't know that was in his background, and I certainly couldn't have known how much great theatre was in his future. But I always sensed that was a home for him artistically.

David was a presenter at The Ovation Awards the first year that I was the Executive Producer. I had followed some of my professional heroes in that position, people who unknowingly mentored me while I ran around making believe I already knew more than all of them combined. Those people included Alisa Fishbach, Larry O'Connor, and Jeff Brown. I have thanked them all privately for their guidance—to which they asked, "What's the angle?" But it is a pleasure to do so publically.

Story

One of my mantras is taking over the lead producer position was that this entire endeavor was about raising the profile of the Los Angeles theatre community. And one of my goals was to have a well-attended, well-covered red carpet. That is the source of all the photos that can spread throughout the world and enhance the image of our industry.

I had walked it early myself, to test it. And was waiting back stage as each of our celebrities arrived having run the gauntlet of paparazzi. Bea Arthur… Peter Gallagher… Annette Bening (gee her name comes up a lot for a person I only met once).

And then my publicist came over and whispered in my ear. "David Hyde Pierce didn't walk the red carpet"

"Yes he did. I saw him in the green room. "

"No, he was totally drained from a full day of shooting, and the hour-long ride to get here and he begged to let him skip it"

I said, "Well… I get it"

"No," the publicist reminded me, "He is one of our biggest names. He is on the number one show on TV. And we have banked this whole evening on the amount of press attention we get. You have to talk to him"

Now I didn't know the guy. I had no idea how he might react. So I started thinking about those mentors. What would Jeff Brown do? Oh, he would clearly respect David enough to leave him alone. What would Alisa do? She would tell Larry to go talk to him. What would Larry do? Larry might requisition a bottle, and

131

offer David a few shots before asking for a favor.

But I ignored what all the people I respect would have done and just flat out asked the guy. I introduced myself, explained how important it was and said "please"

The actor answered that that day had been so draining that we were already at his bedtime and our show hadn't even started yet.

So I did what any producer would do. I said, "Pretty please?"

So in some combination of class, or a direct challenge, or resignation, or duty, he said he would do it on one condition.

"Sure, whatever you need"

His condition was that I walk down the red carpet with him, as his date.

Now he did *not* use the word date, and was *not* flirting with me. He can do much better. I think he just couldn't face it alone and figured if I'm the one making him endure the horror, I should share the burden.

So we did.

He answered every question and we posed for every picture.

And despite the fact that I knew every photographer by name, and that I was the freakin Executive Producer of the show, there appeared a picture in the paper the next day of the two of us with a caption that read, "David Hyde Pierce at the Red carpet for The Ovation Awards with unidentified friend."

Which implied something.

Lesson

Holy crap, my wife puts up with some nutty stuff. But the lesson that applies to you, dear reader, is the idea of the simple direct approach. There are countless tales in this book of my creative cajoling. Sometimes it is successful, sometimes it leads to disaster. That all comes very naturally to me.

But despite my history, the great majority of instances call for a direct explanation and request. Would you be willing to? Here is the reason, please and thank you.

No one will ever invent a simpler or more successful approach.

Chapter Thirty-Five
Bill Murray

Background

Remember that story about how my friends and I met a bunch of girls from California in New York and went out to visit them? Well this happened on our very first visit. It was the fall of 1980, during our senior year in high school. *SNL* was the fuel behind our youthful sense of indestructability.

We were five wild and crazy guys.

And this was our chance to not end up like Mr. Richard Fader from Fort Lee, New Jersey.

And meeting Bill Murray could have jump-started something amazing. But **nooo!**

Story

We were well aware of the Ramones. We were from New York. New York is punk. We hold these truths to be self-evident. That not all music scenes are created equally. They are endowed by their creator with certain inalienable rights, among these are that New York is punk, and everything else sucks. Does that invoke the proper amount of self-righteous bullshit of teenagers who think they know everything about music?

But that being said, we were horny stupid 17 year-old boys. So when the group of pretty girls said, "Let's go to the Roxy and see X. They're the greatest band ever. They invented punk," we all said yes. We also would have said yes to bathing in French fry oil at the Fatburger in Westwood had they offered it... because we were 17 and the girls were pretty.

The opening act was the Flesheaters.

They screamed like an industrial thrash metal genre that was born decades later.

Our heads and ears hurt, and I was probably pissed that I had spent seven dollars on seeing *this*.

Then X came on.

And each one of us instantly got it. Where the Ramones were retro fun punk that sought to consciously remind you that music used to be good. Where the Sex Pistols both extolled and lived within the excess of anarchy. X wanted to tell the stories of L.A. with the poetry of a Paul Simon, a little of Debbie Harry's style sultry defiance, and leave you... Ah... breathless.

But none of that is part of this story. It is just a little mood setting.

On our way out of the club after the show, we were trying to remember where we parked. Another door opened that was part of an adjacent, related, private club called *On the Rox*. I have no idea if anyone else walked out of that door. Maybe a hundred people did, maybe nobody. But there was this group of three people who came out together.

We identified one as Lorne Michaels, one as Laraine Newman, and the third as Bill Murray.

Decades later, you know that Murray is an eccentric who does wacky stuff like crash people's weddings and sing with the band, or hang in the broadcast booth of a Cubs game. But his stardom was new then and his public persona was yet to be determined.

So we stood next to him for approximately forever, way too afraid to actually speak. They were waiting for their valeted car. We were standing there like lamps.

And then one of us. I know it wasn't me... maybe it was Mitch... said, "Excuse me Mr. Murray. We're huge fans. Can you take a picture of us?"

"Yeah, whatever."

So the whole group of us gathered against a wall, and Bill Murray snapped a picture of this magical week in our lives. We all still cherish that picture (well, the boys do, I'm sure the girls were over it in a week). But in retrospect it is odd how in the moment, not one of us, not even Murray, thought it was bizarre that we didn't ask him to be *in* the shot.

Lesson

One lesson is to strike while the iron is hot. We should have asked Murray to join us (and Newman, and Michaels) but the other lesson is about the unique nature of individual moments. That photo would not be more preciously held to our hearts had they posed for it. Photographs evoke memories. And that moment helped define our teenagehood. It's the experience and the memory that hold the value. Not the photograph.

And that holds especially true today where every

person walks around with a camera in their phone and instantly posts a hundred pics a week to a million people. Living life trumps photographing it.

Addendum

I took my daughter, when she was about eight, to see X in concert. She agreed to go willingly because the opening act was Bow Wow Wow and she really likes "I Want Candy"... Mostly because she really likes candy.

But I am stupidly proud that my daughter saw X and Bow Wow Wow for her first show and not some crappy boy band that she wanted to marry because of their hair.

Chapter Thirty-Six
Gwen Stefani

Background

I'm not sure what level of detail I'm comfortable sharing. But my daughter is adopted. Her birth Mother lived in our house for several months before her due date and we accompanied her to the delivery room at Cedars-Sinai in May 2006.

Story

The labor was long and painful. It stretched out over parts of two days. I would give you the details but there weren't any celebrities involved in the birth process. So it is a bit off topic.

Anyway, the biological mom was comfortable with my wife being in the room, but I waited outside in the hallway. And that was more than fine. I really wanted a baby, but I was really not so demanding about being there at the moment of birth. I was happy to be present a few minutes later.

From the hallway I remember calling my brother, who already had three kids, and saying these exact words which I had planned for months "I am in the club." And he said, "What the fuck are you talking about? What club?"

After I explained and hung up, another maternity patient arrived, a young girl who looked like a 1940's Betty Grable and was with what I presumed to be her husband. She was being pushed in a wheel chair and he walked alongside. I certainly was not paying attention to them, but I must have been staring in their direction because the guy said, "Hey."

And they looked *real* familiar.

So I assumed they were someone I knew, and started talking to them that way. "I didn't know you guys were having a baby."

And he said, "Then you were the only one."

Which still didn't register with me.

So we talked for a few minutes, both thinking we knew the other, and actually discovered some mutual friend, "that must have introduced us at a party or something"

And the wife pulls him along and says "C'mon Gavin."

We wave goodbye and the story ends.

Except of course, it doesn't.

I called the mutual friend and asked "Hey, I'm at Cedars having a baby and I ran into this guy Gavin who knows you. Where did we meet? It's bugging me."

"Idiot. That's Gavin from Bush, and the girl is Gwen Stefani."

He was right about the identity, and the idiocy.

So what did I do?

I run radio stations, so I called the one I was running at the time, Playboy Radio. I called in to a live show, and said, "I have a huge celebrity scoop. We are the first news outlet in the world to be able to say that Gwen Stefani is in labor at Cedars Sinai and…"

Boy I felt like the guy who broke Watergate. I was Woodward *and* Bernstein. And this was going to bring a ton of attention and acclaim to our underdog of a station.

But no. We had no publicist to brag about our scoop. We had no social media at the time to document our victory. We had no reputation for celebrity gossip so nobody picked it up. And worst of all… nobody in our audience cared at all.

But Kingston James McGregor Rossdale was born May 26, 2006, the same day as my daughter. Same time, same day, same place. And a couple days later when the press found out… it sucked.

Luckily I was *distracted.*

Lesson

What the hell was I thinking? If the press wasn't on to them, then no doubt (get it?) they had worked really hard to try to have this child without the fanfare and flashbulbs.

And I, who would have gained nothing from ratting them out, jumped at the opportunity. There are times in life when you need to put yourself into the other guy's shoes. I didn't want my special moment to be a public affair and clearly they didn't. And if there was any one person who should have understood at that moment—it was me, as I was going through the exact same life milestone.

I'm glad my effort failed. Sorry, Gwen.

Chapter Thirty-Seven
OJ Simpson and OJ Simpson
(Guest appearances by Howard Stern and Joan Van Ark)

Background

There is a good possibility that some of you have never heard of OJ Simpson. So let me explain who he was. Simpson was a Heisman Trophy-winning running back at USC who went on to star for the Buffalo Bills in the NFL and set rushing yard records while becoming a household name.

You knew that?

Oh, well after that he became a celebrity spokesperson and an actor in quite a few high grossing films.

You knew that too?

Well I bet you didn't know that he was also accused of murdering his wife and her friend in cold blood.

Wow, you must be a news junkie if you heard all of those stories.

Story

Part one of the story takes place on the opening night of a play I was producing in Hollywood. It was actually an evening of two, one-act plays. There was little remarkable about the production. The theatre was small and the actors were talented but not particularly well-known with exception of the off-stage voices which were provided nightly by two of the world's greatest voice actors Billy West (*Ren and Stimpy*) and Bill Farmer (Disney's Goofy)

But we were sold out for most of the run before we even opened. How did that unusual occurrence take place?

One of the performers, the driving force behind the production, and the main investor, was a woman named Nancy Sirianni. Nancy was married to a man named Jackie Martling. And Jackie was the head writer of *The Howard Stern Show*. And this was when Stern was reaching his peak audience—somewhere between 10-16 million they would say at the time.

Periodically Howard would say something on air to goad Jackie like, "Why is your crazy wife running around Los Angeles trying to be an actress? What's the name of that play she is wasting her time on?"

And Jackie would be driven insane trying to defend his wife against the onslaught of the entire Stern team. And then they'd get Nancy on the air to tell Howard to leave Jackie alone. And then Howard would insult them both individually and as a couple, before mentioning the show a few more times.

Nancy put up with it because it sold tickets and spread her "brand."

Jackie, I imagine, put up with it because it was his job to put up with it, and because the money being spent on the play mostly came from his earnings.

Howard put up with it because it was entertaining for his audience and, partially, because he knew he was helping.

After six weeks of rehearsal we were ready for our opening night, June 17th 1994 with an 8:00 p.m. curtain.

As the cast and crew started filing in a little after 6:00 p.m., they all said something along the lines of, "Did you see this car chase thing?"

I hadn't, I was working.

And then, "The cops are chasing OJ Simpson all over L.A."

My response was, "Who cares?" That was intended to be rhetorical, and was unintentionally naïve.

Nancy came in and said, "We have to cancel the show. OJ Simpson is leading the cops on some kind of crazy thing and nobody is going to come to the theatre. They're all going to be watching."

"Calm down," I said, "This is L.A. We have a car chase every other day. Our show doesn't start for a couple of hours and nobody is even going to remember the chase by then." It's a wonder they didn't give me a Nobel Prize there and then.

We expected the audience to start arriving about 7:30, maybe 7:45… they didn't.

Turns out *everyone* was glued to the TV watching the White Ford Bronco, and AJ Cowlings and so on. I don't think many people assumed yet that OJ had killed a couple of people. Though his lawyer, the original Kardashian, read what was obviously his suicide note at a press conference.

8:00 p.m. We have exactly three people in the audience as OJ is pulling up to his Brentwood home. Nobody wants to do a show. Everyone wants to watch OJ. So we did.

8:30 p.m. Two more people have shown up and now we have a portable TV leaning on one of the theatre seats and we're watching OJ instead of performing. Just before 9:00 p.m., the cops have him down at Parker Center and...

We performed the show as an "extra dress rehearsal" and returned people's money.

Lesson

Celebrity giveth and celebrity taketh away. That production had merit. Which included Bill Freiberger's direction and the acting of Jude Prest and Jeff Rothpan. And it wouldn't even exist without the money that came, albeit indirectly, through Howard Stern. And it doesn't get the ticket sales and notoriety that it achieved without that connection.

But as easily as those celeb-based victories were accomplished, so were they vanquished when another celebrity decided to make an ass... a murderous ass... of himself on live TV.

Story
(Part Two)

Part two of the story took place on October 3rd 1995. We, the producers of The Ovation Awards, had scored a coup that we hadn't done previously, and I don't think has been accomplished since. Our nominee announcement ceremony was going to be broadcast on live TV during the local morning news shows.

We rented a hotel ballroom, and filled the seats with celebrities who could read the announcements, because the TV crews were only coming if we promised names they recognized. And, of course, we had everything worked out weeks in advance. Chose the day, time, venue every little detail was thought through.

Until one person said, "Hey, what happens if they decide to read the OJ verdict at the same time?"

You would think that after that last story, I would have taken greater precautions to make any event OJ-proof.

But a month out, what were the odds that the verdict would come in that *week,* much less that day, or that hour.

Wouldn't you know it? The bastard got me again. October 2nd, Judge Ito announced that the jury had reached a verdict, but with the Rodney King riots fresh in L.A.'s memory, Ito was delaying the announcement in order for the authorities to prepare for whatever might happen. Yes, the next morning, October 3rd, at 10:00 am.

In order to get our celebrity presenters to stay committed to attending, we had to promise that we would have a TV available so they could watch the verdict before we held our press conference. I'm glad they were willing to show up at all now that we had lost hope for TV cameras.

Something bizarre and unexpected happened the

morning of October 3rd 1995 (aside from OJ's acquittal). The TV cameras *did* show up. And they positioned themselves strategically around the room… as the verdict was read. Yeah—it's TV in L.A. and they knew this was a great place to get instant real-time celebrity reaction.

I will never forget how at the reading of the words "We find Orenthal James Simpson, *not* guilty," Joan Van Ark faced directly into a camera, hands on her cheeks Macaulay Culkin *Home Alone*-style and mouthed the phrase "*Oh my God*!"

None of our announced nominees were featured on the news, but our show must have gotten a hundred mentions.

Lesson

Celebrity taketh away, but celebrity giveth something back, sometimes.

And I don't begrudge Joan Van Ark one bit. The deal had been set up for us to use her, to use her good name and draw attention to our cause. When the tables turned, she was able to use us a little.

That's the game we're playing, so you can't begrudge the other players from wanting to score some points too.

Addendum

About a year later, Joan Van Ark became the first, and still the only, actual celebrity to recognize me in public. I was walking past a café in Santa Monica where she was having brunch and she actually stopped me. Maybe I'm just an easy mark, but I was pretty touched that she kinda sorta felt she knew me. So Joan, I'm sure you're reading this—you are forever on my list of favorite show business people.

Chapter Thirty-Eight
Justin Bieber

Background

Justin Bieber crashed my birthday party. This story doesn't really need much background, but I'm going to throw some in just so I can drop another name. My wife's brother is one of the semi-original Mighty Morphin Power Rangers. He played the unforgettable, irrepressible, and handsome as all get out, Latino heartthrob, Rocky DeSantos for few seasons. Rocky was mostly the Red Ranger, but for a little while he was blue. No single color could contain Rocky!

By 2012 Steve Cardenas (Rocky had a real name) was long passed his Rangering days and had opened up a Brazilian Jiu-Jitsu studio in Burbank. I started bringing my daughter there for lessons when she was five or so. Steve's girlfriend at the time had the other half of the building and she was a yoga instructor. So while my daughter took lessons on tapping out older boys, Michelle was teaching me to love yoga. And I did, immediately.

Story

So for my birthday that year I invited my entire staff, about 50 people, to join me for 90 minutes of crazy hard yoga right smack dab in the middle of our workday. About a dozen took me up on it. Most of the ones that did were the ones who didn't have structure-specific jobs. And by that I mean, I walked into a yoga studio with a dozen Playboy Playmates.

Most had taken a yoga class before, but not one of us could keep up. Michelle runs a very challenging class. Now my birthday is in August, so now we are walking back out into a 96-degree summer day carrying an hour and half of sweat with each of us, and someone said, "Let's take Farrell to lunch for his birthday!"

You would think Playmates would be so vain that they would not want to be seen in public like this. The truth is that they care deeply about their appearance at public events, when representing the company and the brand. But generally, they tend to dress down on the average day because—this sounds ridiculous, but it is true—when you spend your whole adult life getting hit on by strangers who have already seen you naked, you get in the habit of trying to minimize that constant harangue.

But sometimes that backfires.

As we pulled into the Olive Garden in Burbank, there was a huge commotion. We heard screaming inside, as if someone is in distress. And out came this group of young men, running at full speed, dressed like hoodlums, being chased by a few patrons. I was immediately sure this was a robbery in progress. So I … uh… got out of the way. It could be dangerous.

And one of our Playmates started screaming, "Holy shit!"

I was thinking she might have been hit, but here were no gun shot sounds. They must have a silencer.

Then the hoodlums ran directly over to a pair of

black stretch limos. Hmmmm. That was not a gang thing, the limos with a waiting driver. Well, maybe the waiting driver, but not with that chauffeur cap.

Then one of the hoodlums motioned for our Playmates to get in the car.

And they're considering it!

So, I asked why?

Turned out this was Justin Bieber and his entourage. The girls, being many many decades younger than me, knew him instantly. At least I recognized the name and knew who he was. I just couldn't figure out why he was robbing an Olive Garden. On the other hand, I knew *exactly* why he was flirting with the girls.

Lesson

Ah, one of the great lessons of life. Even when all the visual cues seem to line up properly. Even if young men in hoodies are running out of a storefront, chased by screaming folks, and hopping into ready escape vehicles, they might not be what they seem.

Bieber probably made more money that year than the entire Olive Garden chain. And I figured him for a kid skipping out on the check—or worse.

Addendum

My daughter is the right age group and is a big fan of pop stars. For some reason, she just has never liked Justin Bieber. She has referred to him by all sorts of unkind terms, since way before she was able to know the literal definitions of those terms. He is, up to this point the only artist to whom my daughter has had such a virulent negative reaction.

Chapter Thirty-Nine
Betty White

Background

Do you know the radio show *Loveline*? It's been around for a few thousand years in syndication at this point. If you know it, you probably think of it as Dr. Drew's Radio show with a rotating comedian in the other hosting chair.

But when *Loveline* started, it was the brainchild of a guy named The Poorman. Poorman was, and really still is, an incredibly talented radio personality. He can be irresistible to an audience. But he also can be so incredibly self-destructive that he hasn't been able to get his career back on track after *Loveline*.

And so when the chance came to work with Poorman, I asked around. Everyone said the same thing, "Don't do it. He's nuts. It will end badly."

So naturally, I did it.

And of course, about three days into the show he hijacks the soundboard and refuses to turn on his co-host's microphone until the board lights up with calls.

And then two days later one of the celebrity guests has his female co-host backed up against a wall in an uncomfortable sexual situation, and instead of interceding, Poorman brought the mics out to the hallway to narrate.

We calmed both those situations down and decided to try and do a second week of the show to see if it was any more... civilized. I understood what Poorman was doing, the sensationalism that he saw as essential to building an audience. But it wasn't the kind of radio I wanted to do.

Story

On Tuesday of Week Two our special guest was Betty White. There are some things we all know about Betty White. One is that she has been around this business a very long time and has dealt with every possible situation, so she can see through you in a minute. And the other thing about her is that she has a wonderful bawdy side to her humor if she is comfortable.

We didn't make her comfortable.

After two perfunctory questions about some project she was promoting, Poorman went right into about ten straight questions about her late husband's penis. Betty rolled with the first one, turned it into a joke about "he was more than man enough for me," and she even put up with the second one.

And then she'd had enough, unfortunately Poorman had not.

It was long and painful and really uncomfortable.

But it was also really rude and unnecessary.

But it also failed as radio in the moment. It wasn't entertaining.

But it also failed as part of a long-term plan because we could no longer get any celebrities on the air, and we didn't have the P.R. (thankfully) to reach out and tell the world that we were mean to a nice person who didn't deserve it.

Lesson

There's something to be said for flying in the face of nay-sayers and building an empire where they all thought was barren ground. But you have to be able to separate that, other people's fears and opinions, from actual facts and experiences they're sharing with you. When every single one of a dozen people said, "This will end badly because here is what happened with me..." that should carry more weight than it did with me.

Addendum

I still have a soft spot for Poorman and talk to him periodically. I wish I could find the right formula to get him back on the air *and* keep him from some of his antics.

Chapter Forty
Holly vs. Kendra vs. Bridget

Background

The years I worked for Playboy was during the era of their E! reality TV series *The Girls Next Door* featuring Mr. Hefner and his three live-in girlfriends, Holly, Bridget and Kendra. And, in my opinion, the reason the show had success was that the three "girls" were displayed as three very different characters.

And they really were very different from each other.

Story

The best way to explain the personalities of the three women is to tell you how I first met each one of them.

I met Kendra first, when they were shooting the pilot for the TV show. Kendra was playing on our Playboy company softball team. And the film crew wanted to capture part of the action to establish her as "the sporty one." She had clearly played some ball before. She wasn't much of a hitter but she really tracked the ball well in the outfield, had a decent arm, and knew how to hit a cut-off man. That's better than most of the guys on this co-ed team. Her mom and her sister were there that day, and despite the otherworldly nature of having a TV show filming you when you were 18 and moving in with your 80 year-old boyfriend... and his other two girlfriends...they all seemed really sweet.

I got to know Bridget quite well for a while when the Mansion (that's what we called it when Mr. Hefner's office called us) called and told me to give her a show.

I resisted because of many reasons.

First, I needed Sirius' approval, I couldn't unilaterally decide she had a show.

Our station was aimed at men and *The Girls Next Door* franchise was aimed at young women. And the station was filled with people who worked their way up. The station was a success because every single person had earned their way in.

Then I met Bridget. She already had a degree in communications, but I didn't know this, so I was impressed that this wasn't just a whim. She showed up on that first day willing to listen to me being pompous about the station *and* fully armed and prepared with pages of notes on what kind of show she wanted to do. We did 88 episodes of that show, changing producers three times, and every single week Bridget showed up with an idea, with pages of notes, and with an infectious smile.

I had certainly met Holly a few times. She had come into the studio. We went to the Mansion for live broadcasts. And we had had a conversation or two. But she never seemed happy. The one exception was when she was on the air with Bridget. I haven't read either of their books. But I heard the three of them took shots at each other. But it looked to me then that Holly's favorite thing about her *GND* days was Bridget.

Who knows? Maybe not. She might have been thrilled. But she didn't seem like it to me. Some people just don't show it on their face. I never knew if she was unhappy to have to do these silly radio things for us? Or with something bigger... or smaller. But she was the one of the three I knew the least.

Lesson

I thought Kendra was going to be a goofy kid. She was sweet and smart. I thought Bridget was going be a spoiled entitled pain in my ass. She was the opposite. I thought Holly was going to be the smart sensible one I could get to know. I was wrong on all three counts.

There's no such thing as real people on TV. There are characters on TV, and people in real life.

Addendum

The funny thing about the three *Girls Next Door* women was that my favorite was the fourth girl, Jessica Hall. Jessica was in a few episodes of *The Hills* on MTV, showed up periodically on *GND* and was Kendra's best friend in real life and on two reality shows. Playboy should have made her a playmate, and Hollywood should make her a star.

Chapter Forty-One
Jesus vs. Gandhi, with an assist from L. Ron Hubbard

Background

I am a devout atheist. Not an agnostic. I am firmly and whole-heartedly living with the absolute assurance that there is no God.

But as an atheist, I am a humanist. Which means I believe that we each control our own destiny, and collectively control the destiny of our world. It means that I believe in the greatness of humanity and of individuals. And I would be foolish to discard the wisdom of anyone who believed that their wisdom was divine.

So here is the smartest single thing said by a few of our fellow humans and the surprising way I came upon them.

Jesus

I was working at a Jewish Day Camp as a counselor in the late 70s, and the very wise men running it used to teach us that we should never tell the kids they were "bad," but that it was better to explain what the kid did wrong and say "What you *did* was bad."

And of course it was explained to us that this was a Christian technique following the words of Christ, because Jesus himself preached that it was right to "Love the sinner, but hate the sin."

As I'm sure you've already figured out, the Orthodox Jews, telling me about Christ, were wrong as wrong can be, factually. This phrase, really this whole idea, never appears in any part of the New Testament.

It's a Gandhi quote from his 1929 autobiography. It's a Hindu principle, not a Christian one. But whether or not Christ *said* it, it still is the kind of Christ-like sentiment that he could agree with, right?

In fact, if you Google it, the first few hundred results are of Christians denouncing the idea, here's a representative one from a Rev. Ken Thomas.

"Hate the sin, but love the sinner," is a quote from Mahatma Gandhi, not *Jesus Christ*. I think Satan twists it and passes it off as a Scripture quotation, to get us one step closer to hating sinners, so that we will chase off as unworthy the very people we were sent to save.

On the other hand, Alexander Pope, in 1717 (in case you don't know, that is not Pope Alexander) said, "Love the offender and detest the offense." Lord Byron—a nihilist on his best day, preached adherence to the concept. And Catholic scholarship traces it to St. Augustine's Letter 211 from the year 424 and the Latin phrase *Cum dilectione hominum et odio vitiorum.*

All of that, to my atheist mindset, is meaningless. I don't care who said it. It turns out, just about everyone said it. I have no intention of taking life advice from Lord Byron. Even before the opium addiction. But I also have no intention of throwing away valuable wisdom because it came from someone who adheres to another set of beliefs.

Lesson

And that is the lesson. Do not discard wisdom if it comes from outside your normal sphere. Where you OK with the idea when you thought it came from Christ, but not when it came from Gandhi? Was it OK from Byron because you think you're a libertine at heart, but not from St. Augustine because he was a symbol of patriarchal suppression? Wouldn't you be better off evaluating the idea based on its merits, rather than its origin?

For instance, I am no adherent or fan of Scientology. But I have friends who are. And one bit of L. Ron Hubbard wisdom they have repeated to me often is, "The best predictor of future events is past events."

I use that phrase all of the time. I teach it to my employees, and I use it to make decisions. I think it is a simple usable truism.

Chapter Forty-Two
Ryan Seacrest

Background

I was going to end this book on the Jesus and Gandhi thing. I mean who could possibly be more powerful and influential? Well, I found him—Ryan Seacrest. At one of my stations I had a host named Tiffany Granath doing an advice show every afternoon. She was gifted at making every single member of the audience feel like they were her best friend. I have never seen anything like it.

Every so often Tiffany would tell us, on the air (so I'm not breaking any confidence here) that she was once a roommate of Ryan Seacrest. As she described it, they were mostly platonic, except when they weren't.

Story

Now this was all before Tiffany married a famous athlete, and before Ryan was a household name. But every couple of months, Tiffany would tell the tale about the time she and Ryan got caught "necking" by the police in a parked car outside Ryan's house.

There's nothing particularly salacious about a single guy making out with a pretty girl. But it is kind of cool when it's a big star and a friend of yours. So we all loved hearing the story.

Nevertheless, she was always very protective of Ryan's privacy. For years she told the story without a name attached.

One day during the second season of *American Idol*, I was out of the office having lunch at The Grove—a high-end mall in L.A. When I looked up from my table, who do I see? Ryan Seacrest with his crew, filming segments. Man of the street stuff, asking people which Idol they were rooting for.

Those kinds of shoots are pressure filled and rushed—always. And nobody wants to be distracted. But there was Seacrest, signing autograph after autograph for anyone who asked. I called back to the studio where Tiffany was about to go on air. I told what was going on and she said, "Put him on the phone with me"

There was no way he would have time, the patience, or the interest, to further delay his shoot by getting on the phone with someone he could call any time of any day. But I nudged in past the teenage girls and said, "Hey Ryan. I have a friend of yours on the phone. Wanna say hello?"

He asked "Who?"

When I said it was Tiffany he practically grabbed the phone out of my hand. He lit up. You could see in his face that he really loved her. And again, don't read too much into that. They were friends. But sincere friends who enjoyed each other's company and were glad to have the opportunity to say hello.

Lesson

The impossible is possible. Is it really possible the story your friend told you about touching Ryan Seacrest in a Trans Am could be true? No. Is it possible Ryan is really as good and decent a guy as he seems to be? No. Is it even possible that he has made it on talent and hard work, rather than dumb luck? No. But every one of those things is clearly true.

Every person who knows him seems to agree, and I saw it with my own eyes. More than once. So when you stare at your TV, bewildered by this guy's omnipresence, and your heart fills with resentment knowing he must have made some dark deal with the devil, just no.

The impossible is possible.

Chapter Forty-Three
Eight Celebrities Who Never Hit on My Wife

Background

My wife Beth is a very private person and doesn't really enjoy having any laundry, dirty or clean, aired in a public forum. And that is why despite the fact that we have been together more than a quarter of a century, she appears so rarely in this book. It is a big deal that she is lending me and you, this list. I'm the one at cocktail parties who walks up to strangers and says, "Hey, wanna hear the story about my shoving match with Lenny Kravitz?" That is just not the way my wife rolls.

Nevertheless she has been in and around show business for three decades and has clearly run into more than a couple of people with names you would recognize. And back in the days where she would sometimes get mistaken for Debra Winger, or Jennifer Grey, there was the ever-present fact that men, especially in Hollywood, flirted with attractive young women. IN this #MeToo era, we know it often went even further than that. But we're not all cads and mashers, as they used to say in the 1930s. But more often than not, men flirt. It is the rule rather than the exception.

But this being a book of positive stories, I hereby present to you a list of ten celebrities who did *not* hit on my wife. There are ground rules to this list. First, obviously, the celebrity has to have had some proximity to her. There's no sense in including Thomas Jefferson and Lord Byron. Second, he has to be a person who doesn't have a chapter elsewhere in the book. Third, my wife has to remember not just not being hit on, but some other interesting thing about the non-event. Otherwise, it is merely a list of names.

George Benson

In the late 80's Beth had just moved to New York as her first big adventure as an adult. She had a couple hundred bucks and a beat-up old car because... that is the cliché of how people show up in N.Y., right? Knowing hardly anyone in town that first winter, she decided to meet a friend at an oyster restaurant along the river for a Christmas Eve dinner.

While she sat at the bar and waited for her friend (probably a date, more than a friend, but I'm more than fine without knowing that detail), the gentleman next to her struck up a friendly conversation. He was an African-American guy, clearly older than her, but similarly without plans on Dec 24th.

Early in the conversation he mentioned being a musician. Who knows whether he was relieved or insulted when she didn't immediately say, "Oh yeah, the *On Broadway* guy!" At least she didn't say, "Wait a minute. You're not Robert Guillaume!!!" (That's a "Benson" joke that was funny in the late 1980s)

Because her friend never showed up, it became

three hours of cocktails and seafood and instant friendship for a lonely young lady who needed a friend at the moment. And no tongue.

KISS

Now this is a strange addition to the list, because KISS, especially Gene Simmons, has a reputation for a legendary series of sexual conquests. How in the world did Beth manage to escape even an invitation to "rock and roll all night?"

She was working as an assistant to a commercial producer in a midtown office. Elsewhere in the building, was a manager (or agent, or publicist, or record exec—who can remember?) of some of the biggest acts in music. Beth's boss was friendly with that whole crowd and the rock stars would stop by periodically to say hello (or hit on chicks or drop acid—who can remember?).

Here's the part that seems perfectly plausible. The KISS guys—usually instigated by Peter Criss—loved to come by and take the girls in Beth's office to lunch. You can see that, right? Rock star walks in and proclaims, "Attention hotties, Lunch is on me!"

But that was all. Time after time it was just lunch. The boys never asked if they wanted to extend the lunch hour a few minutes and see his platinum record collection. Never asked any of the girls for their phone numbers. Never said, "Come back stage at my show tonight" Not even "Wanna watch me put on my demon make up?"

William Shatner

Shatner clearly belongs on this least, since he never did anything the least bit tawdry or forward when they met. But still, there deserves to be an asterisk next to his name. Because maybe, he might, if only…

Another of Beth's early jobs was running a teleprompter on countless TV shows both in New York and L.A. If you don't know, a teleprompter is a machine that replaces cue cards. The script is projected on screen and the operator scrolls it line by line, hopefully at the same rate the performer is reading.

Beth was working the teleprompter one night on *Evening at The Improv*, a syndicated standup comedy showcase. On this one particular evening (at the improv) Mr. Shatner was the guest host. And during a break in the shooting, he came over and sat down next to Beth's workstation.

She was kind of nervous and spoke first to break the ice. She decided to mention that she had recently experienced some of his performance skills, because, well, she had. In fact two nights before someone had played her William Shatner's infamous album. It's a weird psychedelic talky version of some kitschy pop tunes. And clearly that kitsch factor was intentional, right? No?

"Mr. Shatner. I just want you to know that I heard your album a couple of days ago and I think it's hilarious"

Apparently Bill wasn't in on the joke.

Or thought his performance was subtly brilliant drama (subtlety always being a Shatner strong suit)

Or maybe the hot prompter girl shot him down before he had a chance to make his move?

166

Who knows? She was just trying to be friendly. But the album reference abruptly ended the encounter.

Shawn Pyfrom from *Desperate Housewives*.

Shawn is a young TV heartthrob, clearly a generation younger than we are. If you don't recognize the name, he is the one who played Andrew VanDeKamp on the show, Bree and Rex's son. I had to look that up—I'm a guy. Therefore I have never seen the show. On the other hand, I'm a guy that has a good brain for trivia, so I know he lived on Wisteria Lane.

Anyway, years before Marcia Cross got her hands on Shawn, Beth cast him in a Halloween themed film she was producing called *Pumpkinman*. A large part of the reason he didn't hit on her, I am convinced, is that he was about nine years old at the time. But because it is better for the drama of this book, I'm going to claim the reason he didn't make his move was that Beth and I got married during the shooting of this movie. And he respected that.

Nonetheless, they did form a pretty neat bond during the filming, as he was clearly a very talented, bright and balanced young man destined to have a really good shot at a career. I remember commenting at the time that his mom was doing a great job with him.

Harry Connick Jr.

This one is a little different than the others. I think my wife would have welcomed some attention from Harry. I get that. He is a good-looking guy who seems really bright and seems to have a good soul. There's a good chance most women would at least be flattered if he attempted to gain their attention.

Alas it was not to be with Beth.

167

The project they worked on was a video for a duet between Harry and Carly Simon. And Beth's recollection is that Harry was quite smitten with Carly. And just so there's no rumors starting, that smittenhood could well just be professional admiration. Carly was a star long before Harry came along, and this was really her project. So no doubt he was watching along in amazement as an idol he respected invited him into her world.

But of all the celebrities who did not hit on my wife, Harry was probably the one whom she wishes had hit on her. Yes, more than Shatner.

Phil Hartman

And speaking of regrets and sadness, even recalling Phil Hartman so many years after his tragic death made Beth cry this morning. She had worked on the crew for *SNL* that made those short films and commercial parodies during the Phil Hartman era.

Let me detour for a second and remind you that it really *was* Hartman's era on that show in the late 80s, early 90s. He stayed on from 1986-1994 and was the backbone of that show during every one of those seasons. He often commented that he wasn't as handsome as leading men, or as brilliant as a Robin Williams—so *SNL* was really the best and only home for his talents.

That sort of humility, decency and realistic worldview was evident to everyone around him. And it is exactly what Beth remembers most from the time they worked together. She talks often about how there were never too many takes that pissed him off. There was never a good idea that he dismissed because it came from the "crew," and there wasn't a person on the set he didn't at least say hello to.

It is a little weird though that when the circumstances of his death are mentioned, and she gets misty-eyed, people ask, "Oh, how did you know him." And her answer is "The Colon Blow Cereal Commercial."

Senator, Secretary of State, and Presidential Candidate John Kerry

Beth worked here in California as part of John Kerry's Presidential campaign in 2004. And this shouldn't be a shock, really. Kerry doesn't have the reputation or the demeanor of the womanizing politician.

Kerry was an interesting guy. A war hero, who threw away his medals. Saved his fellow soldiers on those famous swift boats but refused to stand up for himself when his heroism was questioned. Rich dude who married a much richer wife, but fought tirelessly (because "tirelessly" is the cliché on how politicians fight) for the common man.

He was the kind of guy who would come into the L.A. area field office and ask people how *they* were. He has the ability in person to make that awkward stiffness be sincere. At least in person. It doesn't work nearly as well on TV.

And Beth didn't really work closely enough with Kerry that he would have had much of a chance to pull something anyway. He might not even have known her name. But we both felt strongly that given the current state of the world, no matter which side of any political fence you might be on, it is good to be reminded that there are actual high powered politicians who don't feel the need to inflict themselves upon whatever woman might happen by.

Kerry's running mate that year was senator John Edwards of North Carolina. He was a different kind of guy. His hitting on my wife would have been much more plausible. But nope, that didn't happen either.

Jason Alexander

Another on-set story. While shooting an episode of that *Evening at The Improv* series, Beth worked an episode where Jason was the guest star. There were some equipment related delays that slowed down the shoot, and somehow Jason and Beth ended up spending most of that time talking on the steps outside.

Yeah, just talking. Well maybe she was smoking. She smoked in those days.

Her recollection is that they talked for hours. Some about a shared history in musical theatre. Some about their recollections of trying to make it N.Y. Just chatter.

And that was the end of that.

Except that a few days later Beth got invited to a dinner party, and who should be seated right next to her? Jean-Claude Van Damme! Naaah, just kidding. Jason Alexander. And she was thrilled to see him again. He was both a nice guy and a famous guy. And she liked the idea of picking up the conversation where it left off.

But it was instantly clear that Jason had no idea who she was. Not in a way that was dismissive or rude—he just literally could not place her. And so he spent a couple of hours giving those awkward generic answers designed to either buy time or uncover further info.

Finally, as the evening was about to end, she saw a look of realization come over his face. He suddenly remembered her and came over to apologize... but not flirt.

Chapter Forty-Four
Cinderella

Background

I once produced a pilot for a radio show called *Naked Bible Study*. Most of the idea, the hard work, and the execution, came from the host, Reverend Bill Freiberger. The premise was that it was simply a Bible quiz show where the contestants were the most unlikely of Biblical scholars. Now, in reality there was much more depth and subtlety to the show as Bill would try to muddy the waters with conflicting Biblical passages or verses that conflicted with what you might consider modern reality.

Story

When lining up the contestants, all I really needed was someone personable, who didn't mind being portrayed as someone who was naked under their clothes. It mattered little if they actually got naked, or if they would look good if that happened. It's radio. And, it didn't matter if they had much Bible study in their background. Bill did that heavy lifting.

Basically I hired models. But we had strict standards. We took the first ones that said yes.

In the opening sequence, the women had to describe themselves. One young lady said that, to our shock, she had been a long time Sunday school teacher at a church in her hometown. Who would have guessed that we would have been lucky enough to find a Bible-thumping bikini model? (Dare I say, the answer to our prayers?)

She was really sharp and was unafraid to defend her liturgical positions from the point of view of a Christian, well, a naked Christian.

After the taping I approached her to thank her for being so effusive and engaged. She was worried that she had been too reserved. She said that she lived in fear that we would ask what she does for a living. I said, "People back home don't know about the bikini modeling?" I asked. "They don't, but really I didn't want to say that my day job is working as Cinderella at Disneyland. They don't want Cinderella doing Naked Bible Study."

Which shouldn't have been a worry because we allowed the contestants to use pseudonyms, and would never have used any information they wanted to keep private. But I understand her caution.

We became Facebook friends. Because that's what you do.

She sent me her demo tape. She was also a singer and planned to transition into songwriting and performing.

And I apologize to you for writing this in a way that feels like I'm setting you up to tell you that that a week later she was diagnosed with painful stomach cancer, was disowned by her family, and died a long tragic painful lonely death. Nope. She is alive and healthy today.

However, what did happen a week later was that her boyfriend got in a very serious car accident. I don't think they were adequately insured, and I know the driver of the other car was most certainly not. There was more than a year of painful rehab before he was able to walk again. And he will bear the scars as well as some physical limitations, for as long as he is on this Earth.

She stuck by him, though they were not married and she had no legal obligation to do so. A lesser person would not have. To pay both the medical bills, and the ongoing cost of living for the two of them (his income stream did not survive the accident) she found a job.

First as a waitress in a strip club. And then because it is where the money is for a beautiful young woman in that club, she transitioned into dancing.

I followed the evolving story on Facebook. Never responding with more than an occasional hit of the "like" button. I watched her process her anger at the other driver, and her frustration with a system that didn't handle the boyfriend's needs very well. I watched as the money struggles caused rifts with landlords and other creditors.

I paid attention as she made veiled references to the burgeoning new career, and why it became a necessary part of her life.

There was a noble Jean Valjean aspect to sacrificing your own dreams to support someone who needs you, and has no other option.

And then her posts became less frequent. I imagined she was either too ashamed or depressed to sparkle on social media for my enjoyment.

And I apologize to you *again* for writing this in a way that feels like I'm setting you up to tell you that that a week later she was diagnosed with painful stomach cancer, was disowned by her family, and died a long tragic painful lonely death.

But eventually the curiosity got the best of me and I sent her a message. I said I was wondering how the narrative with the boyfriend played out. Guess what?

They are still together and very much in love. She is still stripping—sometimes in L.A., sometimes in Vegas and thinks it is the best job she has ever had. She says her life has never been better and she was extremely touched that I reached out.

And all of this story played itself out over merely two years in the young lady's life.

Lesson

If there is one thing that life is, it is a roller coaster. The twists and dips are unexpected and scary and thrilling. Sometimes they make you laugh, sometimes they make you vomit. But every roller coaster has those people down on the ground, the other patrons of the park, staring up and being vicariously petrified and innately jealous of your ride.

Here's the chronology. Sunday school teacher, bikini model, Cinderella for Disney, musician, desperate girlfriend, caretaker for a loved one, waitress, dancer.

175

Try less hard to define people with nouns, like the ones in the list above. Often they are temporary. Try using adjectives.

Footnote

I've met a lot of strippers over the years. It is an occupational hazard of being in the radio business and dealing with some adult brands. I have probably had conversations with at least 200 of them. Most of them were charming when in work mode, and a less shiny version of charming when they weren't.

I don't think I could tell you the name of a single one of those young ladies. Oh I could run through the litany of cliché stripper names and I'm sure they would apply. But as I close my eyes and try to match a name with a… let's say, face… I can't.

And you're probably thinking, "Because strippers are disposable members of society and their jobs are not respected."

But think about this, do you remember the name of any specific barista you've encountered? I don't know the names of ladies on the board of my daughter's pre-school. I couldn't name a professional bowler.

Just something to think about.

Chapter Forty-Five
Blind Item Number Six

Background

In 2016 I decided I wanted to start blogging about sports. It seemed like the way best way to learn a little more about the technology in Internet broadcasting and what that world is all about. It might seem like a strange thing to embark upon at the same time I was writing this book. But I saw them as wholly separate enterprises because the subject matter was so different.

The blogging is for a CBS-related sports site. Though I can't really tell you what my relationship with the site is, I can tell you that I am so proud to be on board, and that I actually had to sign an agreement saying I wasn't a CBS employee.

It's really a position that affords neither remuneration, nor prestige.

On the other hand it does allow me to be told by a software algorithm when too many of my paragraphs are more than the average reader's 50-word attention span, or when more than 20 percent of my sentence are in the passive voice, or when (and this one is my favorite) I use too many "stop words."

But it does allow me to pursue two passions—

sports and writing. I think everyone else on the staff is just about half my age, which I love. They're on the site testing themselves and seeing what their lives might hold. And so am I.

Story

One of the silly features on my blog is that I enjoy looking through the comments sections of *other* sports sites and seeing where arbitrary posters claim to have some crazy insider info. And then I do a "What If..." blog extrapolating out the alternate reality of what some random poster threw out to the world to get a little attention.

Yesterday—really, as I'm writing, this happened yesterday, I saw a comment from a person who claimed that he had a friend, who had a cousin, who worked with the wife of a professional athlete. Furthermore, the wife had been depressed because the athlete has been told by the team that he will be traded in nine months. He was told, according to the story, the day of the trade, the team to which he will be sent, and what is coming back for him. Additionally, since the GM felt bad about it, he signed him to a contract much longer and more lucrative than the player deserved.

If you know anything about sports at all, you know that is not a realistic scenario. The list of impossibilities in the story is huge. Trades are almost never agreed to that far in advance, players aren't told about them, and certainly not details about both sides of the deal. And the thought that the GM on the old team would sign the player to a giant deal as a reward?

Not happening. Pure bullshit.

So I wrote my blog post mentioning this cocka-mamie story, including the part where the wife was crying and depressed, and explored the "what if" scenario for the rosters of the two teams.

And within five minutes of the post going live, I get an email from my editor explaining that he had to rewrite the passage about the wife. Her doctor had contacted him and said something along the lines of the woman was actually clinically, depressed, and it was irresponsible of us to exploit her private pain.

Lesson

Sometimes the preposterous is true. There really isn't any logical way Donald Trump becomes President of the United States—and that alone is no endorsement or indictment of the man's campaign or his presidency. We simply do not elect people with that resume and that presentational style. Until we did.

But also don't elect people of color, so there's no realistic expectation that Barack Obama could have won the Presidency, right? Expect that we did.

And that is pretty much the same mindset that lead me to a false conclusion. Guys who spout off on internet chat boards about hearing something from someone who knows someone who heard something—are just plain full of crap. If it smells like poop, it is most likely poop.

Also, if you don't mind me pointing out another lesson—which is so painfully hard for me to learn—people get pissed off by all kinds of things you didn't intend as hurtful. So consider your words more carefully. I don't think I ever would have posted that line in the blog, and maybe not written the blog at all, if I had stopped for a moment to consider the implications. That I was putting into publication that a very specific person, who I do not know, is clinically depressed.

Forgetting momentarily that I took the legally protective measure of quoting someone else *and* using those buzzwords like "allegedly," I helped spread a story that either was false and didn't deserve to have seen the light of day, or was true and was the personal business of the individuals involved.

Despite that fact that the intent was free of malice, the result may have caused a person in pain to suffer incrementally more. And worse, a person who did not choose to become a public figure. Had any of that occurred to me, I may well have decided not to write or publish that blog *or* might have approached it differently.

Addendum

I have three friends that I know of that have tried at some point in their lives, to buy a professional sports franchise. I do not know what meaning to ascribe to it this, but all three told me about their desire to purchase the team during the negotiation process. All three made me swear to secrecy because "if this got out it could cripple the negotiations."

But all three times the information was already public.

And then when each of the three failed to get control of the team, they all refused to talk about it.

Chapter Forty-Six
Oklahoma City Bomber Timothy McVeigh

Background

Buffalo NY. It wasn't a particularly nice place when I was in college there in the early 1980s. It's windier than Chicago, snowier than Denver, and colder than a well digger's ass, as Tom Waits might say. Those are the permanent conditions. But 30 some odd years ago it was also an old world rust-belt city dependent on dying industries. The city felt like FDR's WPA completely overlooked it for new works projects, and that everyone since had followed suit.

The football stadium had steel benches in frigid cold temperatures, and the baseball stadium was called, "The Rock," condemned, and then revived as the decrepit pit Robert Redford's team, The Knights, called home in *The Natural*. Unemployment was high, racial tensions were high, and the city seemed smaller like a combination of watered down beer and mullets.

Oh sure, it had lots of good things too—but they don't fit my narrative.

It was a perfect breeding ground of dissent and rebellion. Where a radical antigovernment terrorist plot was inevitable.

181

Oh sure, it was also the breeding ground for some now famous delicacies like Buffalo wings, and some not-so-famous ones like Beef on Weck. But that doesn't fit the narrative.

Youth is naturally rebellious and frustrated. Youth is more energy than direction. And so it searches for a release. Young men who saw the world as closing around them might surely buckle under the strain. They might see the opportunities afforded their fathers not available to them and scream out in the dead of night. Or maybe they would walk the desolate streets of a hobbled hometown 'til they find kindred spirits among the boarded up windows.

For they are those abandoned storefronts. Once full of hope. Now sealed and concealed. Holders of secrets and anger.

Story

And this is where Timothy McVeigh and I met and shared intertwined destinies. For while it was McVeigh who sulked along searching for compatriots in the underbelly of America. I too sulked along a path. Aimless, halfway through a college experience I was not immune to escapism.

So while the path McVeigh walked was the angry path toward murderous rage, I would look for a new mall every day to walk in when I skipped class.

There was a mall out near the town of Pendleton that I liked quite a bit. Free samples in the food court, and attractive local girls in the clothing stores. With mullets.

It was the first place I ever saw a Guess store.

Guess was a very aspirational, fashion forward brand in those days. At least for us common folk. So I would often stop there and try on an item or two. There was a jacket I especially liked. It was shaped like a short black bomber jacket, but was fabric rather than leather. And had a grey denim midsection.

No, "bomber jacket" isn't really a clue as to where this is going.

This one particular day there was a new salesgirl. And she was stunning. Beautiful and flirty and fun—and likely to make you buy anything you expressed even a mild interest in. I won't describe her physically because, well, I'm in my 50's and it'll seems creepy to go on about how hot a 19 year-old girl is. Don't you think?

I didn't buy the jacket, it was way out of the price range of a student—at least this student. Purchase wasn't a realistic option. But I talked a good game. I usually do. And in one of the very rare times this has ever happened in my life, she slipped me her phone number.

A little piece of paper with her first and last name, the phone number without area code, and a scribble in the corner that might have been a heart… or the result of her trying to see if the pen worked. But I'm going with "heart."

Yep, I stared so long at that sliver of paper that it is etched in the brain.

And kids, let me tell you something. Back in my day there were no cell phones. I couldn't text her that it was cool to meet her, say we should hang, and fill it with emoji's and LOLs. The drill went like this. I had to wait to get back to the dorms where I had access to a phone. I had to seek out moments where there was enough privacy to call a girl and ask her out. And then and I had to call her at her parent's home and say things like, "Good evening. My name is Farrell and I am calling to speak to so and so, I was wondering if she is available?"

Now that I am the father of a daughter, I would welcome the return of such a screening process. But as the college kid with a crush on the girl from the mall, it was overwhelmingly humiliating. But there was no other path to success.

I called and got through her dad—who sounded like the angry "don't date my daughter" dad from every movie. Then met both parents when I picked her up to take her to dinner. Which, by the way, I also couldn't afford. But I liked dates where you can get to know each other and I thought it was classier than the alternatives.

We went to a wine and cheese place at a mall. A different mall. But you know, attached to the exterior of the mall, not the food court. And we had a lovely evening that I don't remember much about. When I dropped her off at home we made out in the car for a while. (Yeah, me.) And when she was about to go inside, she said "Wait, there's something I want to give you?"

And you *know* what I was thinking it was in the car, after making out, with the hot girl from the mall.

But instead she gets out of my car, walks to her car, opens the trunk, and gets out a bag to hand to me. It was the jacket I had tried on the day we met.

Now that jacket cost more than the dinner for two I had just bought. So it was pretty awkward and I wasn't really comfortable. And I said so. "You really shouldn't have bought me that. I don't think that…"

"Don't worry," she answered, "I stole it."

If I was quicker thinking, or more mature, perhaps I could have just said, "No thanks." But I took it and said good night.

Don't get me wrong. No saint am I. I wore the thing to admiration and praise among some friends, and ridicule from others due to the jacket's puffy and not fully masculine appearance. But I wore it nonetheless.

The girl and I spoke on the phone a few more times, even planned another date. But she made it clear that she already had a "real" boyfriend. Not that you can't make a decent future with an adulterous kleptomaniac, but it does present challenges.

So away she went and all I was left with was the jacket, and the paper with her phone number. Which I put on a bulletin board in my bedroom with other numbers I received in bars, malls, trains and clubs.

End of story. So what about Timothy McVeigh?

About a dozen years later, McVeigh and his buddy Terry Nichols decided that blowing up a Federal building in Oklahoma would… You now what? I am not even sure what they hoped to accomplish. Wikipedia says they were mad about Waco and Ruby Ridge.

It didn't hit me when I first heard his name. Tim McVeigh.

Until one news report mentioned that he was from Buffalo, N.Y. Then I started paying more attention. He didn't actually live in Buffalo they said, but a suburb called Pendleton.

The girl from the Guess store was from the same

town… and had the same last name… and, in fact, Timothy had a sister with the same name, around the same age, as the girl I had dated.

I don't really know if it is a coincidence, and in that very heavily Irish part of America there are many McVeigh's. I don't know whether the girl who claimed to have stolen the jacket was the one convicted of illegally sending her terrorist brother a few hundred rounds of ammo.

Lesson

There may not be any connection here at all. I haven't tried to find out, don't really know how, and frankly, don't see what gain there would be from the endeavor. But the lesson is quite clear. No matter how hot your loins may burn in the instant, people who are stealing you things on the first date probably don't make good mates.

First dates are traditionally when we hide our warts and proceed on best behavior.

Stealing for date one could lead to, who knows what, maybe eating gluten by date four? Maybe sneaking in my dorm and unmatching all the sides of my Rubik's Cube. No, it isn't funny. One hundred sixty eight people lost their lives. Thousands more grieved for them. And maybe, someone I once made out with in a car, had her entire existence shattered by that bombing.

Chapter Forty-Seven
Five Celebrities Who were Nice to My Daughter

Steve Cardenas

Chronologically speaking, the first actual celebrity to be nice to my daughter was my Brother in Law. He was the Original Red Ranger on the *Mighty Morphin Power Rangers*. When he was doing the Clark Kent thing, incognito on the show, the character was named Rocky DeSantos.

But that's a cheap one. How much of an accomplishment is it when an uncle is nice to his niece?

So let me tell you a Steve-related story. There's a pretty lucrative business out there in just being a celebrity. And Steve makes good use of that network of trade shows and conventions where fans would want a chance to meet an actual Power Rangers.

Sometimes, when those conventions are in L.A. we'll go and say hello.

I remember one about five years ago in Hollywood. A pretty small one in a hotel near where the Academy Awards take place. And it wasn't comic book or superhero related—it was a convention featuring TV stars from the past. Steve was from the pretty recent past, others were stars from decades earlier.

Bernie Kopell was there, dressed in his outfit as the doctor from *The Love Boat*. But of course we wanted to talk more about his days running the evil communist secret spy conglomerate called KAOS from the show, *Get Smart*. And in the next booth was Valerie Harper from *Rhoda* and *The Mary Tyler Moore Show*. She had been pretty public about some life threatening health issues, so we were thrilled to see her looking so good.

When we got over to that side of the room, Bernie and Valerie were chatting away as though they were old friends, and maybe they were. Clearly catching up was taking precedent over signing autographs for what seemed like a bunch of dudes who were then going to hawk them on the internet.

My daughter was there with two friends. They were all probably in the eight to 12 year-old range then. but when the other dad who was with us explained that we didn't really want autographs, but we just wanted our kids to see that the people they love on TV are real, and decent, and charming, the kids became the focus of the conversation. The three girls talked to the two TV stars for probably longer than anyone else at the convention, and came away... hungry for pizza. What did you expect? They're kids.

Aiden Starr

Aiden Starr is a fetish porn performer, a professional dominatrix, and a natural inhabitant of the literal and figurative places your mother warned you about. (And Aiden is bright enough to scold me for ending her description with a preposition). We don't often travel in the same social circles, but the dom and I have a professional relationship... wait! I mean to say that for a few years I paid her to come in for a couple of hours a week. Wait!

Nah, she was a host on a radio station I was running. But we talked at length whenever she was there about life, the adult industry, the intersection of medicine and the law, the psychological profile of some of our common "friends," or whatever else was the topic of the day.

Some people who dom for a living are a pretty scary sight, and live within that visual character 24/7. Aiden looks relatively acceptable for polite society if you should happen upon her somewhere. But the people she dates are often gender-fluid folk who use their flesh as an artistic canvas. More than once I have had to ask her if her friend was male or female, and inevitably I would be scolded for limiting her to two choices.

One thing my daughter and I enjoy doing together when we have a free day is taking some sketchpads to the museum, and recreating some master works, horribly. It's a thing.

One bright shiny afternoon we came out of the Los Angeles County Art Museum's Japanese Pavilion and my daughter stopped dead in her path. "Dad, there's a freak show, a scary freak show, coming right at us." So I looked.

It was Aiden and the "person" she was dating at the time. By putting the word, "person" in quotations, I wasn't try to imply anything negative about the androgyny. Only that between the make-up, and the piercings, and the tattoos, and the Mad Max thrift store apparel, it was hard to see evidence of humanity.

And my daughter was shocked to learn that the reason they were headed for us was to say hello. To *me*! It was the exact conversation you, or anyone else, would have had when unexpectedly meeting a work associate at the museum.

"How's your weekend?"

"Did you see the Infinite room exhibit?."

"Don't you love the Metropolis?"

They weren't overwhelmingly, or going out of their way nice. Just social, cordial regular nice. Which was a good lesson for my kid.

Noah Rubin

My daughter took up tennis right about her eighth birthday. It replaced Brazilian Jiu-jitsu in the rotation of expensive extracurricular indulgences which I could barely afford. Roaming through Facebook one day, I noticed that the son of an old high-school friend had been a tennis prodigy at Wake Forrest and was now joining the professional tennis tour.

So I wrote to Noah's mom and asked for some advice on getting started as a tennis parent. Aside from the kind words and guidance for me, Noah was generous enough to send my daughter a package of stuff—an autographed picture, some kind encouraging words, etc.

We go out of our way to watch him when he has a televised match. Our favorite so far was a long battle against the legendary Roger Federer at the Australian Open. My daughter draws inspiration and encouragement from the connection she feels to Noah.

And that has value much more than commensurate with the amount of time and effort he put in.

Goofy and Porky Pig

We do a fundraiser for my daughter's elementary school each year where I spend a weekend teaching kids how to be radio hosts. Their "final exam" is to interview a celebrity. The parents clue me in a month early as to what the kid might like. Sometimes it's a wide range like "sports." Sometimes it is very specific like "the hosts from *Hack My Life*." Sometimes it's truly bizarre, like "Falconry."

One year there was a child who was very much into cartoons, so I found her the two gentlemen who layer the voices of Goofy (Bill Farmer) and Porky Pig (Bob Bergen). And I can usually get the celebrities in and out within 20 minutes. They're all super busy and although the money goes to a school, it's not quite like the *Make a Wish Foundation*.

This particular year, an NBA player got his days confused and didn't show up. Well Goofy and Porky stayed an extra hour—making them each late for appointments—just so that one kid wouldn't go home without having interviewed a celebrity.

You won't find two more generous souls than Bob and Bill.

Robin Preiss Glasser

My daughter's favorite author, when she was in first and second grade, was Robin Glasser, the creator of *Fancy Nancy*. She also liked a book series about a pig that goes to Venice Italy on vacation, and lots of the more obscure Dr. Seuss books. Oh, and the Mo Willems classic *Don't Let the Pigeon Drive the Bus*!

But the *Fancy Nancy* series were the books she identified with most closely.

When my daughter was about seven, Ms. Glasser was doing a reading of her new book at Children's Book World in L.A. and we decided to go and listen, have her autograph a copy, and bathe ourselves in the haughty cultural experience of a book reading.

She couldn't have been sweeter, any more engaging to all the girls that gathered, and was even shockingly candid about her relationship with her co-author.

We stayed later than most, or longer than most, and actually had a cup of tea with Ms. Glasser. And my daughter still remembers it to this day.

Chapter Forty-Eight
Five Famous Places That Taught Me the
Lessons Necessary to Write This Book

I saved this chapter for late in the book because it explains so much of what comes before, and because it is cheating. In naming five famous places that taught me lessons that helped me write this book, I take the risk of deviating from the formula. So let me state, unequivocally, that if a sufficient number of readers complain about the nature of the chapter, I will rewrite it to reflect famous names instead of places.

Mitchel Field

Mitchel Field on Long Island is the place made famous by Charles Lindberg. Lindy's famous flight, when he became the first person to solo from New York to Paris, originated in this patch of swamp out on Long Island. It was just a few miles from where I grew up.

Of course I was there a half-century after Lindberg's flight, and in the early 1970's an arena sprung up which now house the NHL's New York Islanders. My dad got season tickets from day one, and we watched them grow into probably the greatest sports team ever assembled. They set an all-sports record with 19 consecutive playoff series wins, won four straight Stanley Cups, set a record for consecutive games won, and did all that with the exact same group of players. Which is really unheard of.

I was in the building on May 24th 1980 when they won the first of those championships on an overtime goal by Bob Nystrom. And for me as a 16 year-old, it wasn't just my favorite team winning. I was that idiot fan who knew all the player's hometowns and their wives' maiden names. I knew every minor leaguer's stats and what to expect from them when they made it the NHL.

But after the elation of seeing them win in that moment subsided, when the jumping up and down and screaming ceased, I remembered a very definite and frankly, defining, emotion that I hadn't expected. "The good guys can win."

Of course with perspective, this bunch of players has no inherent moral superiority to another group because of jersey color. But forget logic. What I internalized at that moment was that the one thing on this earth, with which I identified most closely, had just achieved their ultimate goal. I needed that.

I was born less than 20 years after the Holocaust, and even if the Allies won the war and Israel was created, those Holocaust stories didn't feel like victories. My parents were divorced. I didn't have a smooth school experience either. This event, these guys I didn't even know, winning a championship, felt like proof that life was a winnable game.

And no, I haven't "won" at everything since. But I do believe in it as a possibility.

The Louvre

I have tried to write this book a few times in the past. And always stopped pretty early in the process. One of the mental images that I used to motivate myself through to completion this time, is the Mona Lisa, hanging so famously at The Louvre Museum in Paris.

This might be the most inspirational work of art in human history. Certainly one of the most viewed, studied and revered. But I don't know if a single other person has drawn from it the same lesson as I have.

When I made my first trip to the museum in 1997, Mona Lisa was in a fairly small room, deep inside the museum. It was incased in Plexiglas, either to ward off thieves, natural elements, or handsy tourists. Outside of that Plexiglas there was a barricade of velvet ropes. Each corner of the erected barricade had a uniformed security guard. And that whole set up maintained an exoskeleton of humanity. There was a constant crowd of 100-150 people at all times. All straining to see the great work. Most, I suppose, were like me; a combination of tourist and pilgrim.

What struck me in that moment was how counterproductive this arrangement was. What value is a work of art when it can never be seen and studied and contemplated? Where is the value in a painting when most of the viewing public sees it for a few fleeting seconds, with huge swaths blocked by heads of strangers? When the colors and textures lose their subtlety through a plastic coating?

And what struck me at that moment was that part of the value of a person's work is in its accessibility. No illusion here that I am creating the Mona Lisa of self-help books. But whatever it is I have to say, the idea is to put it in a way that it can be shared.

Niagara Falls

The phenomenon I am going to describe to you about the falls is not unique to me. In fact, before I visited there, every person and every guidebook gave me this same bit of knowledge. However, I am going to present it to you as though it was a revelatory moment for all humanity, because that is the best way to describe how it affects this book.

As you drive from Buffalo toward Niagara Fall on Niagara Falls Boulevard (Highway 62) you might expect to see the touristy honeymoon bungalows that you heard about growing up. For those of you not born in the Northeast, or not born before 1980, you may not understand this reference.

This was the cliché honeymoon spot for loving young couples, probably right up into the 1960s. I had heard about it on TV and in movies. And certainly a natural phenomenon like the Falls, which provided hydroelectric power for most of the Eastern seaboard, and the backdrop for Nikola Tesla's great experiments, and countless legends of daredevils and suicidal idiots going over in a barrel, would be an awesome sight.

But as you start to get close, even as you enter the town of Niagara Falls, New York, you don't see the kind of hotels you dreamed about for your honeymoon. There are establishments with cheesy names like "Sherry and Mack's Crackalackin' Honeymoon Shack" and a log cabin motif-ed place called "The Water LOG Motel."

Most looked more like abandoned sharecropper huts than honeymoon villas. There might have been a quaint kitschiness to it if it were just a matter of style choice. But no, there was also a very unappetizing feel to the dozens of places that lined the roads.

And when you finally reach the Falls and park your car, you realize the immensity of the white noise created by the Falls. Millions of gallons every second come crashing down a thousand feet. The air, your clothes, and every other object are ensconced in mist. Soggy, salty, cold mist.

But of those majestic Falls, you can kind of see them from the viewing rail, if you strain your neck and lean over.

The tourists next to us opened their book, and even there the omnipresent wetness made the pages stick. I heard them say, "Book says it's better from the Canadian side. Wanna try it?"

Oh yeah, that **is** what everyone told me.

On the Canadian side the first thing you see is three brand new luxury hotels. No establishments leftover from the set of *Deliverance*. And the Canadian viewing platform has a breathtaking view that leaves you in awe of nature's power. In fact, from there, you can even hop into a boat called, The Maid of The Mist and ride through the afterglow of the water that has fallen. It's a tremendous experience.

Same Falls. Completely different experience. And that is another thing I kept in mind. I expect those few celebrities mentioned in this book who actually remember the incidents, may remember them very differently. But the book isn't historiography and isn't intended as a thorough examination of pop culture. It is what it claims to be—an accurate depiction of my perspective of events and how they changed me.

Texas School Book Depository

I was in Dallas, Texas to cover the Super Bowl in February of 2011. I got there about ten days before the game and about two days before my crew. One of the main reasons that the NFL chooses mostly warm weather cities for the big game is because they want warm weather. Really, it is that simple.

Warm weather means more tourists, going more places, spending more money. And it means the world's attention is focused on that city looking warm and inviting as the rest of America is in the fourth month of frosty frustrating winter.

And Dallas, Texas isn't like Miami/Phoenix/San Diego. But it is warm. It never snows there. Maybe once per decade.

Needless to say, the day after I arrived, with a suitcase full of warm weather clothes, a three-day long blizzard arrived in town. Dallas was utterly unprepared. There wasn't enough sand to ice the roads or enough plows to clear them. Every day the temperature would go up to about 35 degrees, just enough to melt some snow, and then have it ice over again overnight.

Hundreds of flights were cancelled every day. The teams were having trouble getting into town. The few taxis that ran, drove five mph. And all the media folks that descend upon a town were stuck somewhere else.

So even though my days were supposed to be jam packed with events and coverage—there was a whole lot of nothing going on. My crew was supposed to be broadcasting daily from a restaurant called something like Big Dicks. But that was harrowing because many of the people we planned to interview never made it to town. And others weren't venturing out. I had a great producer on the team who scrambled and covered.

But I was worried. To clear my mind I tried heading over to the Texas Book Depository. That's the spot from which Lee Harvey Oswald fired the shot that killed President Kennedy. It's a museum now. A macabre tribute to a horrific moment.

As I stared out the same window Oswald had stared out, and listened to the provided audio of the news coverage of the day, I was struck by the ability of the news corps to quickly pivot when the story of a visit became an assassination, and then a man hunt, and then the murder of Oswald…

And it hit me.

I was so worried about how to tell the story of this Super Bowl in the midst of this blizzard, that I missed the obvious. The blizzard is the story. And that is a notion I had to conquer to effectively create this book. The focus in't on Springsteen and Capote and Sinatra. They are simply characters. The lessons are the stars of the stories.

Avenida De Revolucion, Tijuana, Mexico

Tijuana isn't what you think. It's a pretty big city with professional sports teams and a thriving middle class. The roads are paved, the schools are in session, and many residents cross back and forth to the United States without trouble or incident every day.

There's a really good chance that when you think

of Tijuana, what you are thinking of is really just Avenida de Revolcion. This is the street, just a few minutes by car from the border, where a dozen children might surround you looking for financial help. This is the street where touristy trinket shops alternate with bars that have dancing girls.

And in those bars, sometimes, the dancing girls alternate with not-really-girls. And strippers of all seven genders are equally likely to lift your wallet or even take a few loose $20s out of a front pocket. Here's my Tijuana debauchery math. Nine out of ten times a dancer who claims to be a girl, is a girl. Pretty good odds. Eight out of ten times she won't steal from you at the club. Seven out of ten times, the drink you ordered from her won't knock you out. Odds are getting worse here. Six out of ten times when you ask her for "extra circular activity" she will answer in the affirmative. And it continues on in a way you can imagine concerning the frequency of getting robbed by her at her place, or by a guy who is waiting for you after you leave, or *la policia* "just happen" to be waiting for you, or coming home safely but with a venereal disease.

I have been down there on more than one occasion, with a variety of traveling companions, and had people in our party experience several of the delightful moments I described in the previous paragraph. Some were painful, some were scary, some were expensive, some were foolishly dangerous.

And we talk about them with joy every time we get together.

Some of the stories in this book are like that. Excruciatingly difficult lessons to learn. But I don't see any reason you shouldn't be laughing at them with me.

Chapter Forty-Nine
The United States Marine Corps

Background

I grew up in the Vietnam War era, and on the apologetically left side of most of those era's issues. That means I grew up in the era when the public image of the American military was at its lowest historical ebb. There are many people today who excuse themselves for the way we thought about our soldiers in those days by saying things like "I hated the mission, but I always respected our boys."

There's a good chance most people saying that are lying. While there were some infamous incidents of spitting on returning soldiers, most Americans never sunk nearly that low. Nevertheless we did think of them as the baby killers, the boys who didn't do the morally correct thing and resist or dodge. We thought of them as hired thugs of a corrupt regime who went abroad to murder for no reason.

And when we were done picking on their morals, we internalized an image of them as kids for whom the American Dream was something they had ridden to a dead end. We thought they were kids who didn't have what it takes to make it in society and took military pay for a few years of sure pay and three square meals a day.

It is hard to imagine today how much of America had so little respect, for the (almost exclusively in those days) men in our Armed Forces.

That started to turn with the first Gulf War. Partially because the all-volunteer military really was exponentially more efficient and proficient than the conscripted version. We couldn't be more proud of both our performance, and our mission, as a nation. In fact the very use of that pronoun, "our" was transformed from painful to prideful. But also because we had grown up somewhat as a country.

The Vietnam War years (which really included JFK's assassination, and Watergate) burst our bubbles of innocence. Most of us learned that war isn't a battle for completion. And that "our boys" make as many mistakes per capita as "our generals," and probably about the same amount as "their boys"

Story

There was still quite a lot of that residual anti-military guy sentiment in my head when I was contacted by someone at Camp Pendleton to participate in something called "The Miss Semper Fi Pageant." It had been around for a few years and it was designed as a beauty pageant for Marine Corps wives. The pageant director, Melanie Wallace, asked if I would be a judge.

So I drove my self-righteous, spoiled little self down to San Diego one weekend thinking about the condescending conversation I could have in my head the next few days concerning these yahoos.

Early in the day I was speaking to one of the contestants. Her husband was a Navy Seal (Pendleton and Mirimar seem to have members of overlapping services) who had been away on assignment for several months. She had a brief weekly window to communicate with him and neither was allowed to mention anything about location or mission. Her husband was away for months and she didn't know where he was or what he was doing.

Later I met a giant wall of a man named Dusty. Though his wife was involved in the pageant, he wasn't going to be able to see it because he was leading his...platoon? In a drop somewhere in the desert so they could simulate war and survival situations. I get why that would be a fun weekend exercise for someone who isn't me. But he was an exceptionally bright, competent, confident guy. Why would he choose this as a career? Even if you enjoy the training, you're training to fight a real war with a significant chance of not returning. Who *chooses* that?

From where we were sitting we could see the ocean. He pointed to the shore. "Sooner or later, someone's landing on that beach. And someone has to die to save you."

If you're like me, you most likely read that as melodrama. It wasn't. It was as sincere, and as matter of fact, as if I had asked why he likes lemonade.

I befriended another of the judges, a Vietnam veteran. His name was Al, but I don't think he would be comfortable with me sharing more than that. He was a guy who saw many tours, in multiple locations. And spent part of every single day visiting friends, brothers, in the local V.A. Not as a "job," but because there were people he served with who were in there.

It had become fashionable again, to find a soldier and say, "thank you for your service" in the years after 9/11. I asked him about that. He said he kept track and in the quarter century between Vietnam, and 9/11, six Americans had thanked him for his service. He didn't resent those who didn't (me), he didn't resent those who were now reborn in their respect for the military (me), he was simply grateful for those six.

Lesson

There are a million worlds within this one we live in. We should not presume to know what inhabits them all. We used to ask, "what if they threw a war and nobody came?" But there are things worth fighting for, and worth dying for. And in 21st Century America, there are scant few of us willing to make the commitment to be willing to die for the rest of us.

What I learned isn't that I should have volunteered. I saw these guys, they are benevolent monsters trained to do the impossible for the greater good. There is nothing I can do to help them, no way I can be of direct service. I was never, at any point in my adult life, qualified to serve amongst these people I believed they were there because they had no options. Now I know, they are better than me.

Chapter Fifty
Bruce Jenner

Background

Yes, Bruce. Not Caitlyn. And that is not meant as any disrespect. But my story occurs years ago. That was before she started living as a woman, or before the public had any inkling that this struggle was going on inside this person. Frankly, I'll come out now and admit that I did not know that this situation existed. The idea that a person was born one gender, but believed they were another wasn't something I had heard of. Except maybe in a movie about multiple personality disorder, where one of the personalities was the other sex.

But that really isn't relative. That's a fluid, shifting consciousness. Transgendered people (I am **so** out of my league here I'll probably get this wrong and be crucified) seem to have an unshaking, constant knowledge of the disconnect between their physical selves and their internal selves.

And I suppose I shouldn't have to say that Bruce Jenner was once accepted as the greatest athlete in the world. But I fear that I do. This person was once the most recognizable face on planet earth. Not too many years ago, that was the most widely known fact about Bruce Jenner's life—the epithet bound to show up in a thousand obituary notices followed by "and he also starred in a movie with The Village People."

Now, not so much. I imagine "transgender pioneer" will be the first listing. Second? "Party to the odd Kardashian menagerie that included OJ's lawyer, magically expanding buttocks, a pro basketball player who overdosed in a brothel, a pop star who constantly interrupted other people's awards acceptance speeches, and led by a visionary who pimped out her young daughter in a sex tape." Olympic decathlon gold medal is a distant third.

And that's all you have to know to appreciate this story.

Story

Beverly Hills is a small town. It has a main street shopping area, pride in its high school sports, And people who all seem to know each other from several other parts of their lives. If you haven't spent any time there, you might be shocked to learn how many residents have spent their entire lives there.

For many years I used to play in a Sunday morning softball game at Roxbury Park on the southern edge of Beverly Hills. We were a bunch of adults—some of us in our 50s and 60s—who enjoyed playing on the Little League field because we could still loft a ball or two over the fence designed to contain kids a tenth of our age.

Many of the guys I played with knew each other because they had coached on that field in the Beverly

Hills Little League. They were always gossiping about which coaches they hated, which umpires were biased against them, which kids got preferential treatment because the Little League Commissioner had a crush on his mom. See? It's just like every small town in America.

Well it turns out, one of the coaches in the league was Bruce Jenner. He didn't seem particularly popular (or unpopular) with these guys. But I was fascinated by the idea that the world greatest athlete was coaching Little League baseball. I had heard the stories about baseball legend Ted Williams not being a good manager because he couldn't relate to someone who couldn't hit .300.

So, I got one of the guys to forward me a schedule that marked when Jenner's games were. I don't consider this stalking. I had no intention of trying to befriend the guy, certainly no thoughts of doing him harm. And I didn't plan on anything habitual. I just wanted to see how this guy related to kids who will never have a small fraction of his athletic talent, or success.

The results weren't surprising. But they were educational. Guess what? He submitted a line up, gave the kids a little instruction, and treated them respectfully. All in all, he was a Little League coach. That's what I saw. The real lesson involves what I didn't see.

But here's what I didn't see. I didn't see that competitive spirit that allowed him to crush the greatest rivals the world threw at him. I didn't see him berate a child for an error. I didn't see him belittle a minimum wage official for a blown call because he had been in the "big time." I didn't see him dismiss another father because he was a union lawyer, or a wedding photographer, instead of a professional athlete.

Lesson

And in a way you probably didn't imagine when I mentioned Bruce Jenner, the lesson here is that what you don't see can be at least as important as what you do see. A person's nature is a mosaic, and never defined by a single word or an idea. And most likely you are only seeing a small fraction of the puzzle pieces that form that human being.

Go back and look at the list of suggested items for Jenner's obituary. On the day I watched him, no gold medal, no reality show, no gender identity issue, no guest starring role on *The Love Boat* had any relevance. They were all part of him. And her. But that whole other dad, baseball coach, decent guy thing was just as defining internally as anything that would headline an unauthorized autobiography.

Postscript

As I said, 20 years ago I was completely ignorant to the existence of transgender people. But that doesn't mean I didn't know any. It turns out that I have known at least three transgender people for more than two decades. I like two of them very much. I think the third is a jerk. Because I was completely unaware that this existed, I was always under what I consider to be a natural assumption—that when people present themselves as a specific gender, they have always presented themselves as that gender. Safe assumption, sometimes inaccurate. I do wonder if I would have treated them differently had I known. Maybe with fear, maybe with disrespect, maybe with condescension disguised as compassion?

Post Script

I may someday write another book. But no, I do not anticipate ever writing a sequel to this book. I simply cannot image living long enough to acquire that many more interesting celebrity stories. So I would like to recommend someone to write it, Tom Dugan.

Tom's face is familiar to you in a hundred TV shows, films, and commercials. He was the sharp dressed man in the diner of that ZZ Top video from way back when. He was a campaign worker in the political comedy, *Dave*. He was a Neanderthal *in Bill and Ted's Excellent Adventure*. He was a lawyer in *Kindergarten Cop*. A cop in *Curb Your Enthusiasm*. And a waiter on *Friends*.

But for the last ten years Tom has been touring the country with one-man plays that he writes and performs in. You should see him as Simon Wiesenthal or Robert E. Lee or Frederick Douglass or Jackie O. Well, he might have just written the last two, and not performed them.

But Tom has the same kind of great stories about celebrities, and the ability to see his own misguided hand in the course of events. Contact him and ask him to include the following: The time he saw Sandy Bullock again, in a Starbucks, 20 years after their friendship had faded away; the time Tracey Ullman fired him from a career-defining gig; the time he walked onto a set and accidentally grabbed the boobs of a major star; the time he snuck in to the Oscars.

Post Post Script

I once had to call my wife and tell her I was going to be late because I was going to a Thai Massage Parlor in Hollywood with HBO's pimp Dennis Hof, the world's most famous male porn star Ron Jeremy, and the even more infamous Joey Buttafuoco.

She asked me why I would do such a thing. And I said, "Because for the rest of my life I can say at cocktails parties, "So this one time I went to get a massage with Dennis Hof, Ron Jeremy and Joey Buttafuoco..."

And I have told the story countless times since.

But there is no backstory, no footnote, and really no lesson. So there is no reason to include it in this book. Except it's my favorite story. So I had to mention it.

About the Author

Farrell Hirsch has lived more lives than any dozen of the proverbial rejuvenating cats you've heard about. Not many people can say they've launched multiple national radio networks, worked with the coaching staff of a major league sports team, executive produced star-studded awards shows, been the co-creator of high-tech start up, written a play that played at Lincoln Center, optioned a TV pilot to major production company, and been the CEO of a nationally recognized not-for profit.

So while he has never been what most would consider famous or wealthy, he is rich in the kind of experiences that make life fascinating and cocktail parties stories riveting.

After moving from his native New York, he embarked on a writing career in the film and TV world with such bizarre highlights as a unreleased Filmation cartoon called Bugzberg, a Kenny G music video, and a board game called "Charisma" created by a guy who's other simultaneous venture was importing Caribbean golf carts to be used on American highways.

All of that lead to career first as a playwright, where he had close to 50 productions of his seven plays everywhere from New York City, to London, to

Stockholm, to Los Angeles, to the Allegheny Highlands Regional Theatre in Ebensburg, PA. The highlights include the two NY productions of his first play *Different States*, which was hailed as "refreshingly real" by the Village Voice, the live televised performance of *The Last Bear* in Stockholm in front of 1500 war refugees from Sarajevo, and his 2001 libretto for the musical *Rockne* - the story of the famed football coach, which had it's World Premier at the Morris Center Theatre in South Bend Indiana in front of a dozen of Knute's descendants.

From there he was one of the people who founded The Ovation Awards, LA's answer to The Tonys. Writing, producing, and lining up talent for those shows for seven years brought him into contact with stars like Charlton Heston, Annette Bening, Carol Burnett, Neal Patrick Harris, Stephen Sondheim, Nathan Lane, Danny Glover, Gwyneth Paltrow, Ben Stiller, and hundreds more.

And then, for no particular reason, since he hadn't really ever worked in radio, he was hired to launch national radio networks, on SiriusXM. The first of these was taking on the inimitable task of turning the world's most visual brand, Playboy, into something viable in the world's least visual medium, radio. The endless drudgery of having to spend countless evenings at The Playboy Mansion parties, of recording Bill Cosby, Etta James, Elvis Costello at the Playboy Jazz Festival, having celebrities like Carmen Electra, Donald Trump, Fleetwood Mac come in the studio, hanging at the Super Bowl with Warren Moon and Lil John was exhausting. And none of that includes, what was quite literally, thousands upon thousand of naked people.

After 15 years of launching more than half a dozen stations, in several languages, he left radio to pursue yet another unscheduled and abrupt life change. Currently Farrell is the CEO of The Muckenthaler Center which has art galleries, a stunning live performance space, and a mission to spend time, energy, and million of dollars every year, to bring arts into prisons, homeless shelters, abused women's facilities, immigrant detention centers, parolee re-entry programs, and anywhere else where there is a scarcity.

Other Riverdale Avenue Books Titles You May Enjoy

A Star Shattered: The Rise and Fall and Rise of a Wrestling Diva
By Tamara "Sunny" Stych

We Love Jenni: The Unauthorized Biography of Jenni Rivera
By Marc Shapiro

You're Gonna Make It After All: The Life and Times and Influence of Mary Tyler Moore
By Marc Shapiro

Annette Funicello: America's Sweetheart
By Marc Shapiro

Welcome to Shondaland: An Unauthorized Biography of Shonda Rhimes

31018827R00126

Made in the USA
Middletown, DE
27 December 2018